HONORING LIFE

Honoring Life

Medical Ethics and Physician-Assisted Suicide

A CONSIDERATION FROM
AN ANTHROPOSOPHICAL POINT OF VIEW

SERGEI O. PROKOFIEFF | PETER SELG

2014
STEINERBOOKS

SteinerBooks
An imprint of Anthroposophic Press, Inc.
610 Main Street, Great Barrington, MA 01230
www.steinerbooks.org

Translated by Willoughby Ann Walshe

Originally published in German as *Das Leben schützen: Ärztliche
Ethik und Suizidhilfe. Eine Betrachtung aus anthroposophischer
Sicht* by Verlag am Goetheanum, Dornach, Switzerland 2010.
www.VamG.ch.

Library of Congress Cataloging-in-Publication Data is available

Print ISBN: 978-1-62148-053-2
eBook ISBN: 978-1-62148-054-9

Contents

Foreword

The essays presented here originated through discussions about "assisted suicide" in Switzerland. Anyone involved in this subject has certainly observed that willingness is increasing steadily to allow or assist human life to end artificially—that is, in effect, to intentionally kill people—in order, it is believed, to save them from further suffering.

Today, our neighboring country, Holland, provides education to certify special doctors for the practice of euthanasia, which is actively discussed there in public; and the number of patients who die each year through euthanasia is published. In Germany, and other countries, there is not this transparency because active assistance in the dying process is generally forbidden. However, from actual experiences it can be surmised that euthanasia is definitely practiced in many hospitals and nursing homes in Germany.

It is often forgotten that in Hitler's "Euthanasia-Decree of September 1, 1939, the motive for euthanasia is specified as *the deliverance from suffering*. It is described there with the words "merciful death": "Reichsleiter Bouhler and Dr. med. Brandt are authorized to have extended power, particularly that of determining as doctors, such that according to critical human judgement, people assessed as incurably ill can be ensured a merciful death."[1]

In the literature about euthanasia, it is widely acknowledged that through this decree the "skewed program" was created whereby not only critically ill people but also the handicapped, psychiatric patients, and finally those indiscriminately determined to be "inferior" were killed by the millions. This decree contained the two essential elements that serve today, just as then, as the fig-leaf of morality:

1. deliverance from suffering

2. "critical," that is, thorough, assessment of the illness condition

Rudolf Steiner had in his library the book *Die Freigabe der Vernichtung lebensunwerten Lebens. Ihr Mass und ihre Form* [Approval for Annihilating Worthless Life. Their Quantity and Form] by Binding and Hoche,[2] which prepared the public for the founding of the national socialists' euthanasia practice. Numerous markings show that Rudolf Steiner had read the book, and it seems most likely that he was referring to this book when in the year of its publication he exclaimed to members of the Anthroposophical Society in Stuttgart: "One can be quite happy if one doesn't really look at the events that happen! One sees today how people allow things to go on by saying: Here and there, this and that happens! They just stand there, somehow without noticing that these things they have heard about have a deep meaning for the continuation of the events. Today, when people hear about important things that must lead to destruction and downfall, they are not the least bit outraged about it. Events are currently happening throughout the world, intentions are spreading through Germany, that people should be appalled about—but they are not! Anyone who is not horrified about these things doesn't have the fortitude to develop a sense for truth."[3]

Anthroposophists, especially anthroposophical doctors, are called upon to take a clear position regarding processes such as are now being practiced in Holland and Switzerland, and to fructify public opinion through the consciousness of humanity that is developed through anthroposophy.[4] May this work by Peter Selg and Sergei O. Prokofieff contribute to this.

Dr. med. Armin Husemann

Director, Eugen Kolisko Academy, Filderstadt, Germany

Rudolf Steiner with medical co-workers in Stuttgart 1924

PETER SELG

Rudolf Steiner's Therapeutic Imperative

Medical Ethics

In April 1924, Rudolf Steiner said to anthroposophical doctors: "In the case of any sick person whom one is trying to heal, even when that person is critically ill, it is the worst thing to think about death. Especially as a doctor, you must forbid yourself to think about the death of the patient as a possibility. The imponderables have such a strong effect. It is an enormously strengthening force when, no matter the situation, you dismiss thoughts about death until the end, until the very end!—and think only, 'What can I do to save any life-forces that can be rescued?' When such a disposition unfolds many more people will be saved than with the attitude that prognoses death. One should never do that. And one must respect such things quite rightly. Then one has earned the courage for healing."[5] Rudolf Steiner's ethical medical statements were "radical"—they came at the beginning of a new healing art that rejected the contemporary therapeutic "nihilism" and turned to methodical therapeutic forces. Anthroposophical medicine, which he made possible, is based on unconditional devotion to life and its forces in an individual's biography. Albert Schweizer, who was a friend of Rudolf Steiner's, spoke about "reverence for life"—and Rudolf Steiner spoke about how the absolute promotion of life-processes[6] must be the focal point of medical consciousness and of every medical treatment, even in apparently "futile," "therapeutically hopeless" situations. According to Rudolf Steiner, even when aspects of an initial "loosening" of the etheric life-body from the physical body can be perceived, which indicates that the moment of death is near-at-hand, the doctor's attention should be intentionally directed to life, and with it to events in the person's incarnation, especially regarding "healing": "One may not say that one should no longer try to heal a person who for days looks as if near death and could die; it could turn out that what has loosened will be reunited. As long as a person lives, one must always strive under all circumstances to heal."[7]

It is known that doctors in ancient Greece did not treat deathly ill patients in order not to ruin their own reputation in the event that the outcome was unsuccessful—possibly also in fear of confronting the forces of destruction and the abyss. But, at the beginning of modern times, Paracelsus, a doctor highly esteemed by Rudolf Steiner, decisively refused this practice. He argued, in the spirit of Christianity, for unconditional therapy and service toward life. Three hundred years later, Christoph Wilhelm Hufeland, Goethe's and Schiller's doctor, wrote: "Whoever has stopped hoping, has also stopped thinking [...], and the ill person must necessarily die, *because the caretaker is already dead.*"[8]

"Every degree of improvement ..."

Rudolf Steiner not only gave numerous anthroposophical medical courses, in which he spoke to doctors about basic questions of medical thinking and treatment, he also energetically supported the doctors in their therapies. Dr. Ita Wegman's first carcinoma patients in Zurich, which she treated with the mistletoe preparation recommended by Rudolf Steiner, had all been labeled by the university clinic as "incurable" or with "unfavorable prognosis." He was also advisor for Ita Wegman's own treatments, and with total medical commitment, he struggled until the very end to save many of his colleagues' lives. He always emphasized that all healing efforts benefited the patients, and that they had to be undertaken with absolute goodwill: "Every degree of improvement that we can procure is an advantage for the sick person. We must never console ourselves with the thought: 'This is karma, and therefore things are taking this course.'"[9] According to Rudolf Steiner, the efforts expended for supporting the life-force, the doctor's healing attitude, and the resulting treatments, further and lead karma "in a favorable direction." Precisely by taking as a basis the perspective of a further life after death and/or a reincarnation of the human individuality, Rudolf Steiner pleaded for doctors' unconditional therapeutic commitment. When the young Dutch psychiatrist Willem Zeylmans van Emmichoven was able to consult with Rudolf Steiner in Dornach during Easter 1921 about his most critically ill psychotic patients, he received specific therapeutic recommendations for each of them, even though Rudolf Steiner told Zeylmans that according to human evaluation no improvement in health would be achieved in the cases mentioned. Zeylmans was surprised—"because conventional medicine does not take the approach that a person would try to heal even though nothing can be achieved."[10] Three years later, in the "Course for Young Doctors" of April 1923, Zeylmans heard Rudolf Steiner say: "This will [to heal] must never be encroached upon. It must always function as therapeutically as possible, so that it can be said: One does everything, even when one thinks the sick person is incurable."[11] The healing efforts undertaken are inscribed in the person's line of destiny. Furthermore, despite the "hopelessness" apparent on the surface, it is possible that many critically ill people can take a turn for the better up until their last breath. According to Rudolf Steiner, it is the doctor's task to contribute to this, so that the chance remains. The real decision about such a turn of events lies not in the hands of therapists, but in the area of human individuality, the human "I." Rudolf Steiner explained that medicine does not treat the human "I," but assists its incarnation in the earthly realm by counteracting difficulties in the physical-etheric, as well as the soul, and therefore removes obstacles to the unfolding of the "I." Also, regarding the *thus understood* freedom and self-determination of the "I," in extreme life-threatening conditions, medicine as an applied art of healing attempts to keep the physiological situation favorable and open for renewed intervention on the part of the human individuality, which, as a result, can allow for new beginnings to arise from unlikely situations.

The Representative of Life

According to Rudolf Steiner, doctors should be representatives of life in medical situations, with the whole of their therapeutic intentions, with their "courage for healing." Doctors stand for the principle of life—for life-*affirmation* and life-*promotion*—and with it, the meaning that exists within the difficult, obstacle-laden earthly biographies whose care the doctors have committed themselves to. Rudolf Steiner has said that it is the doctor's responsibility to stimulate and awaken healing forces in difficult situations. Through the doctor's "healing intentions," the fractured life- and recovery-force of the patient can be re-established and unfolded anew, not through missionary words, but through presence in the dialogic sphere of two human individualities. So far, failing therapies—especially in the psychotherapeutic area—occur in conjunction with a patient's lack of "motivation for therapy." Rudolf Steiner was a realist and knew the circumscribed problem: the primacy of the "therapeutic imperative" (H. Albonico), which he kept intact, but determined that the primary responsibility for therapy was not in the patient's (often sick and/or designated as ill) will, but the doctor's. The following should effectively embody the will to heal and the principle of life: "When those who are sick [...] simply are brought to the point where, through the doctor's individuality, they sense how the doctor is imbued with healing will, then they receive an impulse that is penetrated with the will to become healthy. This confluence of healing intention and the will to become healthy plays a tremendously important role in therapy ...."[12]

In the sense of Rudolf Steiner's understanding of illness and therapy as he introduced it, a patient's death-wish, as well as a suicide-wish or will, can be seen as a part of, or an expression and result of, a serious illness. This "wish" can evoke psychological empathy, as it can be understandable and justifiable in various situations in light of the circumstances of a patient's life and consciousness. However, the ultimate disposition over life is not granted to us—being neither creator nor consummator. One's life is not a possession and does not belong to oneself personally—no matter how much this contradicts the post-modern feeling of autonomy. It is a loaned property; the doctor is forbidden in the strictest sense to cooperate in its destruction or relinquishment. The—inherently sensible—perspective emerging in the second half of the twentieth century of a "treatment order" articulated by the patient cannot hide the fact that the doctor within Rudolf Steiner's medical ethic is not in the (singular) service of the patient's consciousness, but rather is committed to the real individuality of the sick person, to whom the doctor is obligated. The sick person's consciousness may strive for and intend death. It is—as consciousness—however, not consciousness in-itself, nor is it definitively at-one with the actual human "I" and its free nature; much more common are the infinitely varied situations in which this form of consciousness is an expression of a temporary emergency. Individual freedom and self-determination is the goal of human life, yet it is by no means a consistently present, fundamental factor; precisely the field of medicine is characterized by situations in which individuals are not the architects of their own lives, but rather the creators of their afflictions. Consciousness in this condition often reflects a desolate nature, as a result of which the life- and incarnation-will of the individuality retreats. Within Rudolf Steiner's medical ethic, the doctor is committed to *this* underlying, temporarily submerged existence of the individual's will, without which no earthly biography can begin, as well as the divine-spiritual world, which "sustains and orders" earthly life, and from which the real human "I"-being originates. The doctor's assistance can be only in service of *life and healing*, as Rudolf Steiner mentioned with unmistakable clarity in his course *Manifestations of Karma* at Whitsun 1910:

> With our normal consciousness we must humbly remain standing by such questions within the world between birth and death. With our higher consciousness we certainly may take the standpoint that even accepts death as a gift of the higher spiritual powers. With that consciousness, however, which should help and intervene in life, we may not presume to represent this higher viewpoint. There we could easily err, and would encroach in an unheard-of manner upon a realm where we never should: the sphere of human freedom. If we can help a person to develop self-healing forces, or if we can help nature itself so that healing occurs, then we must do it. Should a decision need to be made whether a man might live on or would be better served by death occurring, then it can never happen otherwise than that *our assistance should be a service toward healing.* When it is, then we make it possible for that human individuality to use his forces, and the related medical help can thereby only be of such a kind that supports him in it. Then it does not affect the human individuality. It would be quite different if we would aid the person's incurability in such a manner that he would seek his further advancement in another

world. Then we would interfere with his individuality and commit it to another sphere of activity. Then we have imposed our will on the other individuality. We must leave this decision to the individuality himself. In other words, this means: We must do as much as possible so that healing occurs. For all considerations that lead to healing come from the consciousness that is justified for our earth; all other measures would encroach upon our earth-sphere—in such cases, forces must intervene other than those that fall within our rightful consciousness.[13]

"... which forms of death will cure people"

In another lecture, in Budapest 1909, Rudolf Steiner stated: "Just let medicine keep on developing so materialistically: If you could foresee forty years into the future, *you would be horrified at the brutal way that medicine will proceed, extending to which forms of death will cure people by means of this medicine.*"[14] This incidental remark was not easy for the audience to understand—and it allows many interpretations today. What does the sentence about "brutal" medical procedures in the future and "forms of death" by which patients will be "cured" mean? Undoubtedly, Rudolf Steiner clearly had in mind the further development of materialistic medicine, as well as the coming technological possibilities for intervention. In 1909 he was already able to foresee spiritually to what extent medicine would be in a situation, decades later, for intervening in physiological human processes, for altering these manipulatively or even replacing them. "Intensive medical" technologies of the twenty-first century enable prenatal diagnostics and intervention, "abortion," as well as extremely early birth; they also enable controlling partial body functions through machine processes, and with it, continuing life under extreme conditions that in earlier times would have meant certain death. Was Rudolf Steiner referring to these situations in which there is an extensive replacement of life-forces through machine respiration, and much more—which are hardly ethically reasonable anymore—rather than therapy attempting to support the life-forces? Was he pointing at conditions of "life" that are merely technologically perpetuated—without the possibility of a cure, of the human individuality returning into the body—and thereby prevent a dignified death? Or was he thinking of quite other "forms of death," which present-day and future medicine have yet to be confronted with? Rudolf Steiner knew without a doubt to what degree modern medicine would take up a spectrum of destructive forces—especially those motivated by the therapeutic goal. The emergence of zytostatic treatment forms, and the associated arsenal of corresponding interventions, occurs in a century in which humankind has learned the possibility of destroying the earth and all life-processes.

Ita Wegman began with her mistletoe therapies in 1917, in the decisive year of World War I and of Central European history. The introduction of mistletoe treatment was the beginning of a new therapy on the etheric level by assisting life and its formative forces. It is an answer to the medical path that, still today, seeks healing in the complete destruction of the tumor process through chemotherapy—as a last hope after numerous, similar treatments—which continues sometimes right up to the last breath of the patient, who often dies suddenly and unprepared.

The healing will, the "therapeutic imperative," emphasized so very clearly by Rudolf Steiner, must be seen and considered in connection with the *methods* suggested by him: the paths of absolute assistance for the life-forces and formative-processes that he recorded and developed, with healing substances that call forth and strengthen the activity of human elements, supported by warmth, light and tone, movement and color, touch and massage. Orthodox medicine, however, which has dominated medical practice, took another path, and has become successful in its own way. At the same time, Rudolf Steiner's healing substances were subordinated over the course of the century; and with this it came to pass that the theoretical discussions begun in the immediately preceding time—at the end of the nineteenth century—about the "value of life," the "surrendering of inferior life to annihilation," the "right to one's own death," "gentle dying," "euthanasia," social Darwinism, and the medical economy were actually put into practice.

In the 1940s, one hundred years after the culmination of materialism, the German medical fraternity became a useful instrument in the National Socialists' plans for domination and death. Doctors, along with attorneys, belonged to the most prominent occupational category in Adolf Hitler's Third Reich. Never before in Germany were there so many doctors serving as university rectors; never before had doctors such politically decisive and influential importance as in the Fascism developed in Germany. In concentration camps, as well as other places, they carried out the most gruesome "research" and made decisions about life and death, about "special treatment" and "selection." "Just let medicine keep on developing so materialistically: If you could foresee *forty years* into the future, you would be horrified at the brutal way that medicine will proceed, extending to which forms of death will cure people by means of this medicine." Already in 1806, Christoph Wilhelm Hufeland wrote the warning: "[The doctor] should not and may not do anything else than maintain life—whether it is fortunate or unfortunate, whether it has value or not, this does not matter to him—and if he once meddles with this consideration in his business, then the results are incalculable, *and the doctor will be the most dangerous person in the state*; for once that line is overstepped, once the doctor believes he is justified in deciding about the necessity of a life, then it is only a matter of step-wise progressions to implement the degradation, and as a result, in other cases, the un-necessity of a human life."[15]

Although originally assisting life, medicine's connection with the forces of destruction and annihilation has become extremely dangerous since the beginning of the twentieth century. According to Rudolf Steiner, this has an occult basis: Both healing processes and forces of destruction reside in the Mercury-sphere; the knowledge about substances and materials that help life can also destroy it.[16] From time immemorial, doctors in the ancient Mysteries knew about the close connection of both spheres of power; since then it has been life as well as its endangerment or annihilation in the realm of this activity of power that determines the special ethics of medicine as well as its initiation character.

The Therapeutic Imperative

The present medical situation is extremely complex, wavering between efforts to heal and various "forms of death." In what situations and to what extent modern medicine's technological aids can be rightly embraced is, and remains, an open question. In singular cases (such as a transient coma condition following apoplexy), these aids can maintain the necessary physiological condition for an individuality's return to independent living, and can therefore be effective insofar as they support therapeutic measures that strengthen the organism's life-forces and protect a person's worth. Under other circumstances, however, the aggressive potential of many forms of treatment is repressively opposed to conditions for developing the individuality. Generally accepted solutions cannot be found for these difficult questions—medicine is, and will remain, an area that needs individual comprehension in the strictest sense. In the midst of difficult discussions, however, one should not lose sight of what kind of healing art was founded through Rudolf Steiner's knowledge as an initiate at the beginning of the twentieth century, what medical ethic is imminent in it, and in whose spirit this appeared. The Rosicrucian saying: "In Christo morimur" was rendered by Rudolf Steiner in the Foundation Stone Meditation as: "*In Christ, death becomes life.*"[17] Intended in this sense, an art of healing struggles to help living, formative, and resurrection processes enter into the regions of illness and death.

Since the first post-Christian centuries, workers in Christian hospices have cared devotedly for dying human beings, accompanying them in a dignified manner and with knowledge about the after-death existence of the human individuality, about the passage—not the absolute end—that occurs at earthly death ("In Christ we die"). Rudolf Steiner held this in high regard. At the same time, it is apparent that his courses for doctors introduced the anthroposophical healing art as a newly founded Christian medicine,[18] its primary orientation being not on care and procedures for accompanying the dying person, but rather on the healing (often successful in hopeless situations) taken from the Gospels ("In Christ death becomes life"). Both processes—devoted care for those who are dying and the continual healing intention of medical treatments—are not contrary to one another, but are complementary, in so far as they are able to respect their appropriate boundaries. It is emphasized that Rudolf Steiner's "Course for Young Doctors" consistently treats therapeutic processes with various possibilities for life-support and recovery, which he described as the specific and sole task of this occupational group. Madeline van Deventer wrote about Ita Wegman, whose special "courage for healing" Rudolf Steiner always praised:[19] "*She never resigned and was often able to win the fight against death. And when that was not possible, one felt how important the healing force was for the dead person's further existence.*"[20]

The Physicians' Oath

(Translated into English from the original text [21])

1. I swear by Apollo the Physician and Asclepius and Hygieia and Panaceia and all the gods, and goddesses, making them my witnesses, that I will fulfill according to my ability and judgment this oath and this covenant:

2. To hold him who has taught me this art as equal to my parents and to live my life in partnership with him, and if he is in need of money to give him a share of mine, and to regard his offspring as equal to my brothers in male lineage and to teach them this art—if they desire to learn it—without fee and covenant; to give a share of precepts and oral instruction and all the other learning to my sons and to the sons of him who has instructed me and to pupils who have signed the covenant and have taken the oath according to medical law, but to no one else.

3. I will apply dietetic measures for the benefit of the sick according to my ability and judgment; I will keep them from harm and injustice.

4. I will neither give a deadly drug to anybody if asked for it, nor will I make a suggestion to this effect. In purity and holiness I will guard my life and my art.

5. But I will preserve the purity of my life and my arts.

6. I will not use the knife, not even on sufferers from stone, but will withdraw in favor of such men as are engaged in this work.

7. Whatever houses I may visit, I will come for the benefit of the sick, remaining free of all intentional injustice, of all mischief and in particular of sexual relations with both female and male persons, be they free or slaves.

8. What I may see or hear in the course of treatment or even outside of the treatment in regard to the life of men that on no account should one spread abroad, I will keep myself holding such things shameful to be spoken about.

9. If I fulfill this oath and do not violate it, may it be granted to me to enjoy life and art, being honored with fame among all men for all time to come; if I transgress it and swear falsely, may the opposite of all this be my lot.

Hippocrates, Ostia Museum

SERGEI O. PROKOFIEFF

The Relevance of the
Hippocratic Oath in Our Time

The Founding of the New Mystery-Medicine

Medicine will become a spiritual science. Just as people knew
medicine as a spiritual science long ago, they will know it as
a spiritual science again.

—Rudolf Steiner[22]

Almost 2,500 years ago, Hippocrates (*c.* 460–377 B.C.), the most
famous doctor of the ancient world and father of scientific medicine, composed his well-known oath for doctors. The complete
text of the oath consists of nine sections. Directly in the first,
there is an indication that what is involved here proceeds from
the ancient Mysteries. The prospective doctor had to turn first to
Apollo, who in the divine world was the supreme example of the
highest aspect of the art of healing: perfect health and harmony
between all human body-soul processes and macrocosmic (spiritual) life. Like Apollo's lyre, the physical body had to be in harmony with the world's great cosmic processes. If there was complete harmony, then a person's earthly sheath was healthy. When
this harmony was disturbed, then the person needed an earthly
doctor's guiding influence. Therefore, the second person mentioned in the Hippocratic oath is Asclepius (Latin: *Aesculapius*),
the great doctor and healer of ancient Greece. He was the son
of Apollo and Coronis, daughter of the Lapith king, Phlegyas.

Asclepius, National Museum, Naples

Instructed in the medical arts by the centaur Chiron, he achieved such perfection that—according to tradition—he even revived the dead. But, because in this way he broke sacred laws, he was struck down by Zeus with a thunderbolt. In the visual arts, Asclepius is represented as a strong, bearded man resembling Zeus, who supports himself with a staff encircled by a winding, ascending snake. (The motif of the staff of Asclepius was later altered and used by Rudolf Steiner as the symbol for Ita Wegman's Clinical-Therapeutic Institute, as well as for the Weleda Pharmaceutical Company.)

Asclepius and Hygieia, Vatican Museum, Rome

With his wife Epione, Asclepius had two sons and two daughters. The sons, Machaon and Podalirius, were both doctors, and helped many wounded warriors in the Trojan War. His two daughters are named Hygieia (Health) and Panakeia (Healer of Everything). The Hippocratic Oath turns to these aspects in its third section.

Every healing can occur from two sides: on the one hand, the original healing forces of the body must be activated, which can lead to self-healing (Hygieia); on the other hand, the healing process can be assisted and hastened through medications

(Panakeia). One can also say that the original qualities of these two women represent the dual will forces that are absolutely necessary for healing a patient: Hygieia, the healing will of the patient, and Panakeia, the healing will of the doctor. Standing before these beings of divine, semi-divine, and human origin with their four healing-related qualities, and also before all other "gods and goddesses" of Olympia, aspiring doctors were to uphold their oath to the best of their knowledge and conscience, and to carry out what flows from this source into all medical situations.

The second section of the oath concerns the relationship of medical students to their teacher, as well as to their children, who also had a right to medical education. This was the result of an ancient Mystery tradition according to which the higher, suprasensory capabilities, which every real doctor possessed in those times, could be passed on only through the stream of heredity, and thus were bequeathed through the blood stream. For this reason, it was necessary for priests in the Eleusinian Mysteries to have their own families, so that the stream of secret knowledge could flow uninterruptedly from generation to generation.

The founder of the medical arts, Hippocrates from Kos (c. 460–377 B.C.), came from an old lineage of doctors that was part of this stream of heredity in which it was believed that, going back fifteen to seventeen generations, Asklepios was one of his ancestors. This meant that Hippocrates' own knowledge could be traced back directly to the founder of Mystery-medicine, whereby he became an appointed and competent representative of the medical art of his time.[23]

Because the old Mystery-knowledge was active at the time of Hippocrates, emphasis was still placed on the importance of the blood relationship-based connection of the teacher and the student, who was allowed to take part in the teacher's oral instruction. However, Hippocrates, who was a contemporary of

Socrates and Plato, lived in a time of transition in which the earlier secret knowledge was to emerge from the darkness of the Mystery temple into clear daylight through the intervention of human thinking. At that time the great epoch of philosophical development had already begun in Greece. Therefore, Hippocrates advocated that every doctor must also be a philosopher. Rudolf Steiner underscored this with the following words: "Actually, one cannot imagine at all why the doctor [he had just mentioned Hippocrates specifically] should not at the same time be a philosopher, and the philosopher coincidentally a doctor" (GA 206: August 6, 1921).

Even when oral instruction for doctors was still closely connected with the old Mystery traditions, the facts show that Hippocrates bequeathed to us several documents composed by or accredited to him, and that beginning in his time, part of the Mystery-knowledge was revealed to a broader public circle.[24] Many priests of the old Mysteries knew then that their time was gradually coming to an end. As a result of the Hippocratic Oath, along with the originally authorized blood-related participants, others were admitted to the oral instruction after they had taken a special oath and signed a written contract with their teacher.

Even after the Mysteries had long since disappeared, Plato and later Aristotle, among others, grasped the old Mystery-knowledge with human understanding through philosophy, and preserved it for the following generations. Hippocrates was entrusted to implement a similar transition in the area of medical expertise.[25]

The fundamental rule for all doctors in the third section of the oath expresses that they may never exercise their art to the disadvantage or detriment of the patient. Doctors must approach the patient entirely selflessly, only in service to the sick and in full consciousness of their responsibility to the world of the above-mentioned gods and beings. For the sick person, doctors were not only the bearers of Mystery-wisdom but at the same time messengers of the higher worlds, the healing powers of which worked through them as physicians.

Doctors must heed the three basic pillars in which the divine-spiritual most strongly appears in human life. These apply to birth (conception), death, and inviolable human worth. Above all, the beginning and the end of life on earth do not belong only to human beings, but also to the spiritual world and its gods. Birth—or conception—and death are the two greatest mysteries here on earth. Therefore, Rudolf Steiner emphasized repeatedly not only the earthly, but also the suprasensory character of these two threshold events of human life.

From the beginning, this knowledge belonged to the most important of all true Mysteries and was also to be applied considerately and practically outside of them. Therefore, in harmony with Mystery-knowledge, doctors had to refrain from interceding especially in the case of abortions[26] and every form of suicide support. Only in this way could human beings achieve the necessary appreciation for the divine laws of life's progression. Because at these threshold situations of human life it was and is a matter of cooperation between human beings and the spiritual world, doctors must orient themselves accordingly and prepare their inner purity and piety, especially when continuing to advance and develop their medical practice. The fifth and concurrently central section of the oath, which speaks about this, forms the pivotal point and lynchpin of the entire text.

The sixth section, which indicates the exclusion of surgical intervention from normal medical activity, directly addresses the third pillar in human earthly life, which is connected with the highest respect for what today one calls human worth. This is a very sensitive area, which is especially not being honored by a doctor when a violation occurs in the sexual realm. In the old Mysteries it was known that the highest spiritual powers are connected with the human reproductive forces, so that any misuse of this knowledge would mean the worst offense against human value and purpose. It is notable that here one was speaking only "about any sexual misuse of women and men, free people and slaves." Children were not at all mentioned in this connection—which is understandable because in that time the Mysteries still governed human life and hardly anyone could imagine such a wrongdoing against the "little ones" and "unprotected ones" in the world. Only during this current time of extreme materialism, with the widespread separation of human beings from an active relationship with the spiritual world, has something so horrible become possible, and in the magnitude that is the case today.

Above all, in recent times, with the increasing disclosures of sexual-abuse cases in the educational institutions of the Catholic Church, and also far beyond that, this issue is being discussed broadly in public. Typically not mentioned in many of these reports and articles, including from the Christian-confessional side, is perhaps the most important judgment regarding this question; namely, what the founder of Christianity Himself proclaimed—as though looking prophetically to our time—about such crimes against children and youth. While I have so far not found this in any of the related publications, the reader should call it to memory here what is contained in the Gospels: "Then said He unto the disciples, 'It is impossible but that offences will come: but woe *unto him*, through whom they come! It were better for him that a millstone were hung around his neck, and he cast into the sea, than that he should offend one of these little ones'" (Luke 17:1-2).[27]

Perhaps some readers may wonder about the exceptional acuteness of this thought. Its full understanding can be recognized with the help of anthroposophy. According to Rudolf Steiner's spiritual research, Christ's forces are directly present in the small child, until the third year of life.[28] Thereafter, they continue to be active, gradually decreasing until sexual maturity.

The existential condition of their activity is connected with the sexual innocence of the child until the time of sexual maturity.

Therefore, sexual misuse of children and youth is an act by which the offender not only works in the most damaging way on a person's deepest nature, but in this way also turns directly against Christ.[29] In the Gospel, Christ says: "And whoso shall receive one such little child in my name receiveth me" (Matthew 18:5). From this it follows that whoever doesn't receive the child and instead causes harm, rejects Christ and becomes His adversary. At work in such a deed is the most radical antichristian force, which uses the person as its instrument. It is none other than the Antichrist—documented in the Apocalypse of John as the animal from the abyss with the human number 666, which in Christian occultism indicates the name "Sorat"—that works through the people who perform such deeds.[30] Through such deeds people become great opponents of Christ, striving to eliminate His presence from earthly evolution in order to establish the mastery of the animal.

Returning to the sixth section of the oath—where the doctor who intends to work in harmony with Mystery-knowledge is forbidden any surgical intervention in the human body—the following viewpoint must be considered. This ban is connected with a deep secret: In ancient times the *form* of the physical body was especially valued; that is, it was considered sacred. The form of the body originates from the macrocosm; it is in-itself suprasensory. It first becomes visible when filled with earthly matter at an individual's incarnation.[31] Rudolf Steiner explains how critical this distinction between form and matter is, in particular, in his cycle *From Jesus to Christ* (GA 131), where it is a matter of understanding the nature of Christ's ascension from a spiritual-scientific point of view. The material of the human body comes from the earth; its form or figure, however, is fashioned during the prenatal period out of the whole starry cosmos by the spiritual hierarchies, which were also called the gods in ancient times.

Friedrich Schiller, who was a doctor himself, felt this connection of the physical bodily form with the divine-spiritual world as though from a memory of old Mystery-knowledge. He brought it to expression in his poem "The Ideal and Life" in the following lines:

Only the body suits those powers,
That weave obscure destiny,
But free from time's control,
Nature's blessed playmate
Transforms above in corridors of light,
The *form*, divine among Gods.[32]

Especially for this reason, because the holiness and deep spiritual importance of the human bodily form was still known in the old Mysteries, no doctor could perform something on a human being that harmed the earthly form, or that could destroy it—for the doctor's task was to heal it; that is, to bring the human being into harmony with the cosmos and its eternal laws. Therefore, other people clearly positioned outside the Mystery-stream were available for surgical interventions, for example removing kidney stones.[33] It is obvious that after the final decline of the Mysteries, no significance was seen in separating surgery from the rest of the doctor's profession. Above all, in the present epoch of the consciousness soul, which has an especially close connection to the physical human body, new perspectives have also opened up for surgery, so that even it, along with all other areas of medicine, could be received into the being of the new medical Mystery-culture.

The penultimate, eighth section of the Hippocratic Oath has also retained its relevance and significance up to our time. It addresses the issue of medical confidentiality. The mental state and medical condition of a patient that is experienced by the doctor through deep insight into the soul and the entire life of the sick person may never be communicated to a third party without the patient's permission. Just as confidential and protected as the sacrament of Confession was, and is still—the content of which must remain a strict secret between penitent and priest—so was the doctor also obligated to be absolutely silent in regard to the patient. For only through such secrecy were the conditions able to be upheld such that in these intimate interpersonal processes, as they transpire between priest and penitent or doctor and patient, the spiritual world and its beings could also cooperate; in the sense of the Mysteries, this cooperation was necessary for healing the soul and body.

With the ninth section the text ends with the strict warning that only doctors who steadfastly comply with fulfilling this oath will achieve success, fame, and advancement in conducting their occupation. By breach or negligence, the opposite will happen. For in the sense of the Mysteries, this oath was not taken primarily for human beings, but before the spiritual world and its gods; and the doctor was to be held responsible even in the afterlife.

*

What Hippocrates had accomplished at the height of Greek culture in transforming the healing profession from the seclusion of the old Mysteries into the clear daylight of the medical profession's public practice was consummated by Rudolf Steiner from a different direction, and in quite another form, at the beginning of the twentieth century, after the dark period of Kali Yuga elapsed in 1899.[34] For although one is able in the spiritual science founded by him to see the activity of the etheric and spiritual-soul elements upon the human physical body, as was still the case in the old Mysteries, it is however in spiritual science, and thus also in anthroposophical medicine, not a matter of something instinctive,[35] as Hippocrates experienced, but a matter of research into the bodily and suprasensory components of the human being, imbued with scientific clarity and discretion, that is the foundation for the new art of healing.

In answer to Dr. Ita Wegman's question about founding a contemporary medicine based on Mystery-knowledge,[36] Rudolf Steiner was able in the last years of his life to accomplish with her a reconnecting of the medical profession to the spiritual world and its beings—especially to Archangel Raphael—and with this a renewal of the old Mystery-wisdom in the area of practical healing knowledge. In this way, the foundation for a new Mystery-medicine was laid through anthroposophy.[37] Today the Medical Section of the School for Spiritual Science at the Goetheanum has the task of cultivating and developing this new medical impulse.

What Rudolf Steiner presented, especially in many professional medical lectures at the beginning of the 1920s, is still valid today as a guideline for the further unfolding of anthroposophical medicine in the world. Rudolf Steiner's inaugural deed in the healing profession is, for our time and into the future, of as great importance as Hippocrates' deed at the height of ancient Greek culture, which had held good for the following epochs of Western history and was considered an incontestable authority until the late Middle Ages.

In this context, it appears to be no coincidence that the maxims of medical ethics that Hippocrates compiled in the pre-Christian fifth century out of the already subsiding Mysteries maintained their full validity among physicians worldwide until Rudolf Steiner's lifetime.[38]

To be sure, Rudolf Steiner never required an oath, or anything similar, from anthroposophical doctors and medical students. However, as Peter Selg has already mentioned in his essay, and as is documented in various publications of the Medical Section at the Goetheanum,[39] Rudolf Steiner cultivated the absolutely highest regard for the principle of life in all its manifestations as the steadfast foundation of anthroposophical medicine. This follows not because of any ideological or confessional requirement, but proceeds from the entire anthroposophical conception of the world and of humanity, which for the first time since Hippocrates has brought earthly wisdom together with spiritual knowledge from the source of esoteric Christianity in a new, modern way, and through this has raised natural science— including medicine—to a true *spiritual science*.

Thus, anthroposophy as the modern science of the spirit and, with it, anthroposophical medicine (which remains a strict science after its permeation by spiritual research) finally abolish the separation between the natural and the moral world-order by re-establishing the connection with the spiritual world, consummated by conscious affiliation with the true source of morality and professional ethics. Instead of occurring in a dogmatic way, this is based on the knowledge of a comprehensive human concept, which in anthroposophy connects the natural with the moral, the physical with the spiritual, the earthly with the cosmic; and thereby makes available to the physician and other professional groups[40] a definite starting point for their practical activity that includes both the natural and the spiritual.

Therefore, in summary one can say: Through anthroposophy a new ethical orientation is given to human life, and to every practical occupational practice, providing a competent knowledge-basis for experiencing the singularity and highest worth of each person, which is anchored not only in the earthly but also in the cosmic-spiritual world. This also enables us to recognize and appreciate today the complete modernity and up-to-date significance of the Hippocratic Oath.

Sergei O. Prokofieff

Physician-Assisted Suicide?

An Anthroposophical Position

What is concerned?

The number of suicides over a specified time can be an indicator of an ailing inner condition of an entire civilization. An increase, then, is a sign that the existing illness in that society is progressing further. Examining our current civilization for this symptom makes it possible to determine that suicides are increasing worldwide, which expresses something about the degree of illness in our current civilization.

What leads to this illness? Here essentially two root factors can be named. One, the increase and dissemination since World War II of materialism, which emerged as a more or less theoretical worldview in the second half of the nineteenth century and during the twentieth century to become the prevailing factor in Western civilization. Today as never before, materialism is no longer merely an abstract theory, but rather has achieved widespread acceptance as an attitude and a practical approach toward life.[41] The second root of our civilization's illness that supports the growth of the suicide rate is lack of real sympathy and true love. As these most important stars in the human moral cosmos increasingly fade, so that negligence and indifference take the upper hand in social life, the forces that can prevent the predilection for suicide in our society are also vanishing.

Albert Steffen reported a conversation in which Rudolf Steiner expressed this fundamental problem of present-day civilization with only two, but decisive, words, which are of special relevance to this whole dilemma: "In order to justify for myself the right to speak with Rudolf Steiner, I decided to present him with a case that I couldn't make heads or tails of. I had an acquaintance (he was of the strictest and noblest character, determined with regard to philosophical knowledge by his commitment to Kant) who had shot himself in the head. He had survived, but the hopelessness that had driven him to the deed continued. He would accept no advice, not even consolation. I admit this often aroused annoyance in me, and I wanted to show this also in the report I gave to Rudolf Steiner. With one glance, he replied: 'More love.'"[42]

One can differentiate three main types of suicide. The first, however, cannot really be designated as suicide, even though it gives this impression outwardly: when suicide is the result of a soul-illness. Rudolf Steiner pointed out in this regard that abandoning one's own life under such circumstances is not really suicide. Even the after-death consequences of suicide, which he articulated so clearly, do not entirely follow in such a case.

In contrast to this is another reason for prematurely ending one's own life, which involves ending life due to "weariness"—because the body or the life-circumstances no longer offer the enjoyment or pleasure that was customary before. In this case, suicide may be committed out of an unconscious egotism, along with a quite materialistic view of life, that is, with complete ignorance of the existence of a spiritual world. Or it may even be out of the egotistic wish to provoke the spiritual world by deliberately resisting its eternal laws. Be that as it may, what Rudolf Steiner has described as the spiritual result of this deed for a person's after-death existence and future earthly life is especially applicable for this type of suicide. Moreover, when egotism is the *essential* motive for such action, the result could possibly be even more severe than is normally the case with suicide.

Between these two is the most common motive for suicide: the wish to terminate forcibly for oneself the often insoluble problems of a bodily or soul nature. Above all, difficult-to-bear physical pain or a momentary impulse of total despair through the sudden loss of one's life-expectations and any hope of a possible solution can, like an alien force, compel a person to such a deed. (This was the case in the above-described suicide attempt of Albert Steffen's acquaintance.) In addition, the inner compulsion of false thinking, which due to apparently irrefutable logic fools a person regarding the assumed hopelessness of a situation, can lead to suicide. This happens through great inner obstruction and therefore requires as prevention the help and loving guidance of other people; and even, when necessary, a doctor must be enlisted in order to protect the desperate person, if that is still possible, from taking the fatal step.

Here—as with every case of suicide—one can and must show the person involved the deepest sympathy in the difficult life-situation, but it is nevertheless important to give full consideration to the objective results of self-destruction as described by Rudolf Steiner.

The following consideration is in no way intended as a moral judgment of such a tragic destiny, but should simply serve to clarify the spiritual background of the observations of Rudolf Steiner's suprasensory research. Above all else, those involved with such radical life-difficulties need the special care of fellow human beings, along with preventive support and medical treatment that counteracts their intentions.

Continuing this description, the three categories of suicide will be considered in their broad-reaching consequences, based on extensive anthroposophical understanding of the human being and the world. Though this is done fully conscious that the objective results of modern spiritual research are not easy to bear for those whom a person has left behind through suicide, only a truthful understanding of the results of such a deeply tragic deed permits finding the ways and means to alleviate the *reality* of the unfortunate person's situation after death, at least partially, through the help of devoted friends who can turn it to good.

Over and over again, especially in early lectures, Rudolf Steiner mentions the difficult after-death experiences of people who have taken it upon themselves to end their earthly life. Such people suffer greatest immediately after their death, because their proper transition to life in the spiritual world, the time necessary for letting go of physical life, is basically missing. Normally, this occurs through an illness or another type of bodily condition that comes about in the destiny of the person in question. "In natural death, the separation of the three bodies is relatively easy. Actually, in a rapid, natural death, such as caused by stroke or otherwise, a separation of the higher members from one another has been prepared for a long time; they separate easily, and the deprivation of the physical body is then only a very small matter" (GA 95: August 24, 1906).[43]

However, because the transitional experiences are lacking— which are often not easy, but nevertheless necessary—immediately after the deed, the soul of the person who commits suicide feels a great emptiness or total hollowness through the sudden absence of the physical body, which elicits a tremendous yearning for the lost entity. "Therefore, we now understand the horrible destiny and the terrible agony of this unhappy person who resigns life through suicide.... It is an awful destiny. The person feels empty and begins a desperate search for the body so suddenly removed. Nothing can be compared with it" (ibid.).[44] This circumstance does not allow for the dead person's soul to enter the spiritual world in the right way, but rather forces it to remain in the spiritual atmosphere directly bordering the earth for a longer period of time. Rudolf Steiner points to this in the lecture of June 30, 1906, by saying: "The most difficult thing for those who commit suicide is this removal [from the physical body] ... an unspeakable yearning for the physical body seizes them, which holds them close to the physical world" (GA 94).

When this happens, there is a danger that the person will be used by certain evil beings for their goals. "It is terrible to perceive human souls who at a certain time in their lives between death and a new birth have become, have condemned themselves to become, servants of the evil spirits of illness and death" (GA 144: February 4, 1913).[45] Furthermore, Rudolf Steiner points out from what moral deficiency during earthly life such a difficult destiny in the after-death period is called forth for the person in question. One finds namely "that in their life on the physical plane they have had a deficiency of conscientiousness and of the feeling of responsibility" (ibid.).

If one looks in the sense of this statement by Rudolf Steiner at the reasons that often lead to a suicide, and which are often also understandable, then one can find—either for those people who commit suicide or for those who support them in this fateful decision, or even for those help them execute the deed—precisely such a moral irresponsibility. This does not rule out the fact that in rare, individual cases suicide can also be karmically determined. For it often happens that a person is altered to such an extent through a difficult, for the most part psychic, illness that the individual can hardly be responsible for his or her deeds.[46] Thus, Rudolf Steiner answered a question about the effect of suicide on life after death, and said that special circumstances in which a suicide is committed under a condition of insanity, that is, executed as the result of a psychic illness, must be looked at quite differently than otherwise. "Already other conditions exist; one must look at the overall destiny."[47]

At the beginning of the twentieth century, Rudolf Steiner explained in a lecture a further motive for a person's suicide, which today, one hundred years later, has undoubtedly become even more apparent. Already in our time—and this will likely increase in the near future—the people following this motive comprise a substantial number of the clients of various euthanasia organizations. In answer to a question that was posed by

Rudolf Steiner himself, he mentions the frequently arising reasons for the decision to end one's life, and then describes the after-death suffering of a person who commits suicide: "It is a terrible destiny. The person who commits suicide feels hollowed out and begins an anguished search for the body so suddenly withdrawn: Nothing can be compared to it. Many people will now say: The man weary of life no longer clings to life, otherwise he wouldn't have taken it. —But this is a misconception, for precisely man who commits suicide clings very much to life; because it no longer offers him the satisfaction of customary pleasures, perhaps because much is denied him through altered conditions, he therefore chooses death, and then the withdrawal from the physical body is so unspeakably difficult" (GA 95: August 24, 1906). Added to the difficulties that the man who commits suicide has inflicted on his own life after death through his deed is the fact that he can be used by demonic spirits, as mentioned above, because his deed stems from irresponsibility to his life and destiny.

When one searches for the true reasons for a withdrawal from life, such as Rudolf Steiner describes above, one also finds in these people—in addition to intensified egotism—a pronounced materialistic attitude toward life. For such people—and there are many today—focus their life on a continual pursuit of amusements and outer enjoyment, which eventually forms the entire content of their earthly existence, so that life is totally senseless for them when this goal appears to them no longer attainable for some reason. The physical body is thereby not considered the creator of soul-processes, but a purely mechanical apparatus, which one simply turns off at any time when it is no longer able to adequately fulfill one's tasks. Inasmuch as people who think and feel in this way don't anticipate anything after death, they also feel no particular moral responsibility toward themselves or for others; namely, for the accompanying doctor who sends them to their desired death.

Now we will explore a few further aspects of this theme in the light of spiritual science. In addition to various statements Rudolf Steiner made about the negative effects of suicide on a person's after-death existence—namely, that it doesn't really solve the problem but only transfers it to the hereafter, and even increases it—a few Christological effects of suicide should be considered.

"Dying in Christ"

The most important information about this theme is found in the essay here by Peter Selg, which indicates that only when higher beings can participate in the death-process is it possible to experience the "In Christo morimur" ("dying in Christ").

This phrase forms the central part of the familiar three-part Rosicrucian saying:

> Ex deo nascimur
> In Christo morimur
> Per Spiritum Sanctum reviviscimus

Which can be translated thus:

> Out of God we are born
> In Christ we die
> Through the Holy Spirit we are resurrected

Rudolf Steiner transcribed this verse, as it appears in the Foundation Stone Meditation:

> In God humankind has being
> In Christ death becomes life
> In the Spirit's universal thoughts the soul awakens.

(GA 260a: January 13, 1924)

In his lecture series *The Inner Being of Man and Life between Death and a New Birth* (GA 153), Rudolf Steiner uses these words to characterize the complete cycle of human life on earth, and between death and a new birth. He connects the healthy life of the human being on earth with the inner experience of the first thought. Only when we become ever more conscious of our relationship to the divine spiritual world from which we have descended through the gate of birth, can we also really appreciate the full meaning of life on earth; it is good for every person to recognize that this is in reality penetrated in every way by divine power and profound wisdom.

The relationship to Christ, which is expressed in the second part of the saying, becomes fully significant at just the very moment of death. Since the event of the Mystery of Golgotha, Christ is connected with every human death as an active and transforming force. Therefore, Rudolf Steiner transcribes this second sentence as: "In Christ death becomes life" (ibid.). Depending on a person's individual karma, the presence of Christ at death can still be experienced in the last moment, so to say, directly on the threshold of the spiritual world,[48] often without the person having the possibility of telling someone about it.[49]

When, however, as is the case with suicide, there is a self-willed intervention in the higher activity of the beings of destiny, which is approved of or even assisted by others, then the possibility for a direct encounter with Christ at the moment of death is withdrawn from such a person, whereby that soul is thrust into a condition of the greatest misfortune an earthly human can ever have. In this regard, Rudolf Steiner has stated that the denial of God is comparable to a physical illness, and the rejection of Christ is a disaster. "Spiritual science must call the rejection of Christ a disaster.... Being able to find Christ is to a certain extent a matter of destiny, something that must play into a person's karma" (GA 182: October 16, 1918). Nothing intervenes as decisively in a person's web of destiny as suicide, a deed that is totally contrary to Christ's activity.

A person who ends earthly life prematurely through suicide and therefore rejects the possibility of dying "in Christ," can no longer experience the full extent of what the second Rosicrucian saying really means: That in Christ the dead will receive new life. This, however, has further and grave consequences for the soul's after-death existence. According to Rudolf Steiner's description in the cycle mentioned, the soul needs the Christ-impulse after death in order to maintain self-consciousness of its own spiritual being until it reaches the World Midnight Hour of spiritual existence.[50] But the soul can take hold of the power of the Christ-impulse only on earth,[51] in order then to take it along through the gate of death into the spiritual world. In this regard, Rudolf Steiner says: Being penetrated with Christ-substance when we are present on earth is what gives us the possibility of maintaining the memory of our "I" until the World Midnight Hour after we transition from the physical body into death. The impulse proceeding from the Christ-force extends that far, so that we don't lose ourselves [in the spiritual world]" (GA 153: April 13, 1914).

When the "I"-consciousness, filled with the presence of the Christ-force in the human soul, is not extinguished before the World Midnight Hour, then in this highest point between two incarnations, a fertilization can occur by the Spirit of the Cosmos, which in the Christian tradition is called the Holy Spirit. Through this, the human soul awakens to a comprehensive overview of its entire destiny, and on this basis is able to shape its next incarnation in harmony with the spiritual world. Moreover, the Christ-impulse—acting as the soul's "I"-supporting force, and carrying the soul within it—strengthens the impulse of the Holy Spirit with which a person is fertilized during the World Midnight Hour to such a degree that in this strengthened form the individuality can be taken through the gate of birth into its new earthy life. This is what is necessary especially today, because the entire future of humanity will depend upon the Holy Spirit flowing into earthly civilization in this way. However, if this does not happen, humankind runs increasingly into the danger of losing the Spirit on earth.

In this way, Rudolf Steiner connects the third Rosicrucian sentence "Per Spiritum Sanctum reviviscimus" with both the soul's awakening at the World Midnight Hour and the possibility of carrying this Spirit-impulse out of the higher worlds onto earth with the help of the Christ-force, so that the resurrection in the spirit can also be achieved in earthly life. "Those who resurrected through the Holy Spirit at the Midnight Hour of existence will also be resurrected when they live into their physical body, when they live into their physical being. They will awaken inwardly when the Spirit arouses them out of the sleep into which they would otherwise be induced by observing only the sense world and by brain-bound thinking" (ibid.: April 14, 1914).

At the end of the lecture cited above, Rudolf Steiner mentions still another result that also comes into being when one passes through the gate of birth into earthly life with such a strengthened Spirit-impulse. Then it will be possible for a person to participate in the greatest spiritual event of our time: Christ's appearance in the etheric.[52] "The power of Spirit that enters into the physical body in this way will bestow spiritual sight, so that the spiritual world may be seen and understood" (ibid.). And the first thing that a person will behold in the spiritual world, when awakened by the Holy Spirit, will be the Christ Himself. Then it will be so: "That people will see the etheric form of Christ" (ibid.).

Suicide is especially tragic when it is done out of inner despair or hopelessness. The karmic consequence, then, is that the special possibility which exists today of encountering the etheric Christ cannot be perceived in such a situation. Maria von Nagy has reported extensively about this in her commendable study of suicide from an anthroposophical point of view.[53] For today the appearance of the etheric Christ occurs most commonly at the point in one's biography when one finds oneself in complete despair and cannot sense the ins-and-outs of one's life. Then Christ can appear as "Living Comforter" (See GA 130: October 1, 1911). However, for those who end their own life just before this relieving event, the misfortune can hardly be greater because the possibility for Christ to intervene in a helpful way is removed.

Maria von Nagy writes in her book: "Our tragic fellow human beings who commit suicide are certainly driven into situations where they know neither the 'ins nor outs,' because they do not know that they should cherish the hope of experiencing the highest thing conceivable; they don't have the energy to wait until the door opens and the 'Comforter,' Christ, appears, but instead they flee from the moment. But one must understand their motives! Those who would throw the first stone at them should be quite certain that they themselves could persevere. The more understanding we can bring to the behavior of such people who commit suicide, the clearer it will be to us that ignorance of the most important fact of Christ's activity is a main factor in their final decision. In this context, characterizing suicide as a great misfortune is justified today."[54]

As a result, when a person makes it impossible to experience the normal after-death process as described, by ending his or her own life, the opportunity to meet the etheric Christ for the next earthly life is also lost, and therefore a further incarnation is needed for this encounter. For as already mentioned above, the perception of Christ in the etheric is directly connected with the strengthening that occurs through the Holy Spirit during the World Midnight Hour, which a person renounces in the case of suicide.

Suicide and the Life after Death

A further disastrous result of ending earthly life by one's own decision is connected with a special secret of death that can be discovered today only through spiritual science. This is that death is considered especially wonderful from the perspective of the spiritual world. In describing this, Rudolf Steiner used more superlatives than anywhere else in his works: "Death is horrific, or at least can be so as long as a person remains in the body. However, when a person has gone through the gate of death and looks back at death, it is the most beautiful experience of all that is possible in the **human cosmos**. For this—reflecting on the passing over into the spiritual world through death— between death and a new birth is the most wonderful, the most beautiful, the most magnificent, the most marvelous event of all that the deceased can look back upon" (GA 157: March 2, 1915). Bright and clear, this archetypal experience of the after-death existence accompanies the deceased on their further path through the spiritual world; it keeps them awake and upright whenever they reflect on the moment of the death of their individual "I"-consciousness. "It [the death-moment] is always present, but it stands there as the most beautiful [moment], as the awakener into the spiritual world" (ibid.).

Why is looking upon the moment of death from beyond the threshold so monumental? It is because through this, one can see one's direct connection with the deed of Christ on Golgotha. "This *resurrection of the spirit*, accompanying the complete shedding of the physical, is an event that always stands between death and a new birth. This is a supportive, wonderfully profound experience" (ibid.). The phrase "resurrection of the spirit" used here is a key to understanding what is essential about this after-death experience. For in it is reflected everything that is described here as undergoing "death in Christ," and "in Christ death becomes life," at the moment of dying. But this must only happen in harmony with the spirit of the whole cosmos[55]; that is, also in harmony with each person's karma, the shaping of which Christ directly participates in today. However, by ending one's own life, one not only falls out of the fabric of one's whole karma, but one also impairs one's relationship with the entire cosmos, with which a correct connection cannot be established as a result of the breaking off of one's life.

Above all, however, because no resurrection force can be active any longer (because one is not in harmony with, but in contradiction to the spiritual cosmos one loses the ability to look back upon the moment of death and experience its awakening character. Thus, the moment of death neither enlightens the one who has died through suicide, nor does it become the source of a new life. What a human soul experiences in looking at the moment of death from beyond the threshold, Rudolf Steiner describes:

> There in the brightness
> I feel
> the force of life.
> (ibid.)

As a result of suicide, it is precisely this which does not occur. Because the moment of death does not illuminate the soul between death and a new birth, the life-force that is absolutely needed by the soul on its further path through the spiritual cosmos to maintain its individual "I"-consciousness is also not awakened.

In this case, the fulfillment of the end of the verse cannot come about:

> I will be
> and make out of myself
> what illuminating power
> radiates into me.
> (ibid.)

Instead, after a suicide the soul feels as though extinguished in the spiritual world because it doesn't find any illuminating power in itself, and therefore cannot out of its own "I" unfold any real life-force for its further path after death.[56]

In this regard, even more is excluded through suicide. Even when one didn't pay much attention to the spiritual world during earthly life, one can to a certain extent make up for it later by looking at the moment of death as described. Rudolf Steiner reports: "A person who otherwise [during earthly life] didn't think much about death, who never or scarcely paid attention to the spiritual world, can receive after death, especially in our time, a wonderful instruction about dying" (ibid.). The person who commits suicide does not encounter such instruction in the spiritual world, but must continue wandering in a lonely way through the spiritual world without understanding and inner orientation.

Through the unlimited working of Christ's grace, as well as through the active spiritual help of those left behind on earth, this desperate condition after death can be alleviated to some degree.

The Relation to the Hierarchies

It is self-evident that all who consider taking their life out of despair, or who have already done so, deserve our greatest sympathy and full inner condolence, even when this cannot be felt regarding their intentions. Here one must have the courage to confess: Through a suicide, even one accompanied by a doctor—whether a person is conscious of this or not—one is helping the Prince of Death, Ahriman, in the battle he is waging against Christ today. Thereby, the evolutionary stream of destiny connected with the entire world, which is woven by the higher hierarchies between death and a new birth, is decisively compromised in favor of Ahriman. This is expressed in the fact that the soul does not enter at the point in time preordained by destiny into the higher regions of the spiritual world, and therefore, for a longer period of time than otherwise would be the case, remains as though bound to the earth-sphere, which lies completely within Ahriman's sphere of influence.[57]

Moreover, beyond the threshold of death, the soul of the person who has committed suicide loses to a large extent the relationship to its own "I"—for after death it lacks the supporting Christ-force, which as we have seen, is connected with the backward-glance experience of the moment of death—whereby the after-death existence proves to be very difficult. Such a soul needs a very long time in order to bring itself into the right relationship with the spiritual world in which it then finds itself, and especially to achieve the necessary independence in it. "When a person commits suicide, he identifies his 'I' with the physical body. Therefore, there arises later a passionate longing for the physical body. He then appears, as if a hollowed-out tree, like one who has lost his 'I.' Then he has a continual thirst for himself" (GA 93a: October 7, 1905).

This loss of relationship to the "I," together with an extreme "thirst for the self," make such a soul dependent on ahrimanic beings, as previously mentioned, whose activity upon the human soul after physical death Rudolf Steiner summarizes in his book *Occult Science: An Outline* in the following words: "In the spiritual world this [ahrimanic] force brings people into total isolation, drawing all feelings of interest only to themselves" (GA 13: p. 287/G).

And it is just this situation that prevents the soul, to a degree, from connecting after death to the higher spiritual world and the hierarchical beings there, whose support and help are indispensable on the entire path between two incarnations.

In order to understand how damaging this can be, contemplate the following meditative statement from Rudolf Steiner, which reveals how in the first three days after death one entrusts one's entire web of destiny to the beings of the Third Hierarchy: In etheric weaving, Angels, Archangels, Archai receive a person's web of destiny (GA 237: July 4, 1924).

Now it is obvious that in the case of suicide, when life is intentionally disengaged at an arbitrary moment, the web of destiny cannot correspond to cosmic laws. For the moment of natural death has already been decided upon long before from the spiritual world (this is also the case for a "sudden" death, for example, in war or from an accident). Because the proper connection with the spiritual cosmos is absent in the case of suicide, the beings of the Third Hierarchy cannot work correctly with the web of destiny entrusted to them—at least not until the point in earthly time occurs of the originally predetermined moment of death.

After a person's suicide, this ensuing fundamental problem for the Third Hierarchy has far-reaching consequences that can show their relevance directly in the next incarnation: For that incarnation cannot be correctly prepared, since it is the beings of the Third Hierarchy who are primarily responsible for continually assisting and accompanying the human soul in the spiritual world until its next earthly birth, and even beyond this point.[58] For the reasons stated, after a suicide these beings cannot link the individual's web of destiny correctly with the spiritual cosmos, the world of the higher hierarchies. Thus, there are quite concrete consequences for the person in the next earthly life. For it is the beings of the Third Hierarchy who also help the growing child to acquire in the first three years of life the three most important capacities of a human being: uprightness of the body (walking upright), speaking, and thinking. The Archai attend to the power for upright walking, the Archangels that of learning to speak, and the Angels that of the capacity of thought.

Rudolf Steiner speaks about this in the following way: "We surrender ourselves in admiration and reverence to these great world phenomena—and here behold the work of the Archai who are active there—while what is experienced between death and a new birth is carried forward in its earthly [upright] form. In how the child produces speech we follow the activity of the

Archangels; and again, in the child's thinking, the activity of the Angels" (GA 226: May 18, 1923).

In this way, the activities of the Third Hierarchy that begin immediately following a person's death (the receiving of the web of destiny) are closely connected with the embodiment of the three original capacities of the child resulting from the prenatal forces, so that with an impairment of the first process the second is also affected. Therefore, as a result of a suicide in one life, it is possible that in the next there will be a disturbance in the unfolding of these three capacities. And inasmuch as these are the foundation for the earthly "I"-consciousness that develops later, this can be an impairment in the person's essential development. This does not mean that all special needs people who have had difficulties arising in early childhood—learning to walk (moving the limbs), mastering speech, unfolding logical thought—that have impaired the awakening of their "I"-consciousness, have ended their lives forcibly in a previous incarnation, but only that a search for the results of such a deed could be focused in this direction.

Naturally, people who are affected in this manner and need special care call forth our emotional attention and love. For only through the selfless help of fellow human beings can they regain a connection to their own karma and thereby also to the entire cosmic network that in the midst of all humanity will be woven together by Christ as Lord of Karma in a new way and in accordance with a higher unity.

The Working of Christ's Grace

The efforts of those who have been close to the unfortunate person can have a significant influence on the consequences of suicide for the following earthly life. And it can be that the person is thereby given the possibility of moving forward, even in the despairing situation in which that soul finds itself after death when it cannot find Christ and thus its own inner peace because what is most important is missing; namely, the right relationship to its own karma—and with this, to its own self. Only through the *grace of Christ*, which is the final means of recovery for the soul, is this possible; for the connection of the soul to its destiny, destroyed by suicide, can only be re-established after death through the power of the Christ-"I". This connection to Christ must, however, be made possible and supported by the active assistance of the people who are left behind. From their own devotion to Christ they create for the deceased a new relationship to Him, whereby the results of the suicide can be alleviated in after-death existence.

In this sense, Rudolf Steiner gave to a mother whose son had taken his life the following meditation for the dead:

> Soul in soul land
> seek the grace of Christ,
> which brings you help,
> which helps from spirit land,
> which also provides peace to those spirits
> that in troubled existence
> are despairing.
> (GA 268, p. 228/G)

One may wish to accompany such a soul by meditating on this verse; through this act of support, such a soul can be led after death to Christ, and once again into connection with its own "I" and with the stream of its karma in the spiritual world. And so for this soul, the work on offsetting the results of this grave deed in the coming life, which would have perhaps taken several earthly lives, becomes possible in a quite different way than would have been the case without Christ's direct help. Through the working of Christ's grace, this situation can be greatly accelerated.

It is significant that Rudolf Steiner's first suprasensory experience was an encounter with the result of a suicide: as a seven-year-old boy in the waiting room of the train station in Pottschach—where he spent most of his time alone due to the various duties of his parents—he had the suprasensory perception of his mother's sister, who took her life in a town situated far from Pottschach. The aunt who had just died appeared to his inner vision with her characteristic gestures and pleaded: "Try now and again to do as much as you can for me!"[59] With this desperate call for help he was given a task that, living alongside his other public activities, remained always in the background and played an important role in his life. One can only guess how many people Rudolf Steiner may have helped in his later life through direct suprasensory vision of their tragic destiny.

The Oath of Hippocrates

At this point we will recall once more the Hippocratic Oath, which has previously been discussed extensively. This oath, to which thousands of doctors swear to this day, contains among other statements: "I will neither give a deadly drug to anybody if asked for it, nor will I make a suggestion to this effect." Reading these words, it seems as though they resound like a great warning directly from the wisdom of the ancient Mysteries to people of the twentieth and twenty-first centuries.

Seeing that this high morality in medicine flowed so clearly and unmistakably from the pre-Christian Mysteries into humanity, these words of Hippocrates should be taken all the more seriously in our time. For we know that as of the twentieth century Christ as Lord of Karma increasingly guides and shapes human history, and we are more and more urged to become His conscious helpers and co-workers in this area.

What is the meaning of this activity of Christ in relation to karmic law? Rudolf Steiner describes the task that Christ has taken upon Himself from our time on in the following words: "That our karmic account is balanced in the future—that is, when we have found the path to Christ [on earth], it is placed in the world order for the future such that our cosmic compensation calls forth the greatest possible salvation for humanity for the rest of earthly evolution)—this will be the concern of the One who from our time on will be Lord of Karma; it will be Christ's concern" (GA 130: December 2, 1911).

Karmic law, as such, continues to exist. What changes fundamentally, however, with Christ appearing as the Lord of Karma are new possibilities for bringing this to realization. For, any deed can be compensated in a number of different ways. Christ chooses the path that leads to the greatest possible salvation for all humankind. To help Him in the way described above will be the most important task from now on for people on the earth. The more we advance in cooperating with Christ toward this goal, the more strongly can karma be freed from the law of iron necessity and become a force of grace that fills life with new light and higher meaning, manifesting in selfless service to humankind.[60] An essential part of this service is our spiritually responsible accompaniment of souls across the threshold of the spiritual world (also in the medical area), so that a premature termination of life will not be [morally] possible. For such an action is only possible when the meaning of the following earthly life is entirely lost. And so, it must be the urgent concern and goal of anthroposophically Christian-oriented support of the dying process and suicide prevention efforts to bring higher meaning back into a person's life, and with this, assurance of the full significance of further remaining in the body, as well as all the powers of karma under the governance of Christ.

Concerning the transformation of karma from the law of iron necessity into the new working of Christ's grace that has begun in our time[61] and will comprise the entire future of earthly evolution, Rudolf Steiner points out the following in the second part of the Foundation Stone Meditation, which he laid into the hearts of the members of the newly founded Anthroposophical Society at the Christmas Conference of 1923/24:

> For the Christ-Will in the encircling round holds sway,
> In Rhythms of Worlds blessing the soul.
> (GA 260: December 25, 1923)

This present karma-shaping Christ-Will answers and resolves many questions and problems with which people are faced now, and will continue into the future.

Christ as Lord of Karma joins together karmic threads quite differently than was the case in the past epochs of human evolution. And this new, still-emerging Christ-imbued web of destiny must not be impeded through human misunderstanding and arbitrary actions.

Rudolf Steiner indicated how concrete this cooperation with Christ in the field of karma will become in the near future: "The more we move toward the future, people will learn that they were united with Christ before birth, that they have experienced His grace, enabling them to clear away their old karma from previous incarnations…. Thus, people in our time will learn that Christ will reveal Himself ever more suprasensibly, and that these karmic threads will increasingly govern the affairs of the earth" (GA 143: April 17, 1912).

From what has been said, one can gather that there is a certain arrangement between Christ and human beings before their birth, according to which they endeavor to live out their karma in the sense of Christ, in order to encounter Him again later and hand over to Him the fruits of their cooperation at the end of their life—at the moment of death. Then Christ can carry these fruits into their coming incarnations for the well-being of all of earthly evolution.

If, however, the encounter with Christ at the moment of death is made impossible by suicide, then the above-described "governing" of the karmic threads by Christ is more difficult. In the same lecture, Rudolf Steiner expressed this dilemma in yet another way. There he speaks about a new love for one's own destiny (*amor fati*) that will grow ever more strongly for a person out of this cooperation with the Lord of Karma. "Thus, one learns to love karma, and then this becomes the impulse to recognize Christ [as Lord of Karma]. Human beings first learned to love their karma at the Mystery of Golgotha" (ibid.).

And conversely: It could even be said that if one rejects one's own personal karma so radically, as in the case of a suicide, one has an unconscious hatred of one's own destiny, that is, of the manner in which it should be connected in this life with the general web of karma in the sense of Christ, and thereby of the way this process relates to one's individual biography.

In order to clarify the present problem, one can use the following comparison as an aid. Imagine that a long time ago a man agreed to meet someone who is important to him at a certain place and time. At the agreed-upon time, however, the person in question did not come, but arrived perhaps when least expected. In this way, those who commit suicide unconsciously turn down the real possibility of the encounter with Christ at the moment of death, and instead appear in the spiritual world when they are not "expected," which is why they cannot at first find Christ.

The resulting situation is especially tragic: As the only one of all spiritual beings in the spiritual world to have done so, Christ alone has gone through a human death and thereby united Himself with *every* person on earth—and further, because of His promise of absolute loyalty toward humanity, also wants to assist *everyone* in death: "And, lo, I am with you always, *even* until the end of the world" (Matthew 28:20). This unshakable loyalty of Christ toward every earthly human being can, however, be rejected. Then such an unconscious refusal of Christ's promise of loyalty could additionally become a rejection of the fact that He suffered death on Golgotha for all human beings, and overcame death for them.[62]

With suicide, the possibility of such an encounter with Christ is, to be sure, not banished for eternity from the person's biography; yet, for several incarnations access to the sphere of Christ as the Lord of Karma is made substantially difficult. For the person's web of destiny—woven by Christ as the Lord of Karma—is damaged, and depending on circumstances, more than one earth-life could be required to bring things into order again. Also, with regard to future incarnations, much will depend upon what conscious efforts the person can and will contribute to re-establishing the web of destiny that had been destroyed. In other words: How far will the person be ready and willing in the future to help balance the effects of suicide in the previous life, in the context of Christ's activity as the Lord of Karma?

The State of Inner Health

The often-stated assertion that suicide is justified—and is perhaps the most radical expression of human freedom—is a fallacy. According to Rudolf Steiner's *The Philosophy of Spiritual Activity* (GA 4), true freedom can only be achieved in thought-activity that is completely separated from physical life and has therefore become sense-free. During an illness, however, and especially when there is great physical suffering (whereby in modern medicine there are many possible means of relieving strong pain) the soul is very closely connected with the body and, therefore, to a great extent not free.[63]

This fact also applies to a still more frequently stated argument for suicide, namely, a life-situation that appears desperate because of the loss of all hope for life. In this case, the person is confronted with an inner bondage by being driven by an external situation into an emotional impasse, so that no other way out of its coercion can be found than to commit suicide. Even for people who are more rationally than emotionally inclined, an iron compulsion can emerge through a sort of thought-logic that can no longer break through its "devil's circle." Thereby, this "logic" also stands in the way of true human freedom just as much as does the emotional despair in the previous example.[64] If the person is able to overcome these thought-based, emotional, or physical constraints, then it is possible to stand as a truly free human being. In order to achieve this, the active help of fellow human beings, and perhaps also a good doctor, is often necessary.

If the bondage caused by a physical condition is overcome by the sick person out of pure spiritual force, then, seen from a higher point of view, one can describe this person as "healthy." In this sense, Rudolf Steiner spoke of the incurably ill poet and anthroposophist Christian Morgenstern (1871–1914), remembering their last meeting before his death: "As I saw him then in his room in Leipzig,[65] it was strange to see just how healthy, how internally vigorous this soul was in the failing body and how this soul just then felt so healthy in spiritual life as never before. That was for me what fashioned the words I later spoke at his cremation: 'This soul testifies so rightly to the victory of the spirit over all physicality!' He had worked for years in bringing about this victory in which he was so closely connected with us through our spiritual science. He achieved this victory not in arrogance, but in total modesty."[66] For, considered from a spiritual-scientific perspective, every moment that a person remains in the physical body, despite everything that appears to speak against it (the discomforts of old-age, emotional suffering, strong physical pain) is a permanent victory over Ahriman as the Prince of Death.

In this sense, to help a sick person actively achieve an internal victory over physical difficulties, even when a healing can no longer be expected, is an important task not only in anthroposophical medicine, but also for any medical effort at all. Such an inner "victory of life over death" reveals the real effectiveness of the Christ-force in a person on the threshold of the spiritual world, and leads to consequences in after-death existence that go far beyond the personal biography of the individual in question, as Rudolf Steiner spoke of with regard to Christian Morgenstern's post-mortem destiny.[67] The poet expressed it thus in a poem composed shortly before his death:

The sick person:
"I often wish to die...
And how thankful I am nevertheless
That I live and suffer here
In the ordered here and now.

If time still remains for me
To reduce some infirmities,
If I never come to rest
I will be better prepared.

If I cannot be active now
I nevertheless help myself,
For what occurs here and now
Will be active in the hereafter."[68]

When Rudolf Steiner was once asked in a private conversation about the situation of a person who had been completely debilitated, he pointed out the exceptional significance of such a life. His words were recorded by an older anthroposophist: "A very sick woman, who lay disabled in bed and had to be fed, aroused such sympathy in a member of the [Anthroposophical]

Society that the member expressed in a conversation with
Rudolf Steiner that it certainly would be better if the sick person could be put out of her misery. Rudolf Steiner replied very
seriously: 'No, every hour she lives on earth is *important* for all
humankind.'"[69] And concerning a person who was very old and
often sick, whereby he became increasingly frail, Rudolf Steiner
reported from his spiritual research the following: "To a certain
degree, from a certain age on, which one cannot perceive with
external senses, we spiritualize the physical earth. We carry spiri-
tuality into the physical earth. ... This prevents the advances of
Ahriman" (GA 183: September 2, 1918).

If a person wants to remain connected to the Christ-impulse,
the argument of so-called "humane release" from great physical suffering cannot be used. This can be gathered from what is
depicted in the Gospels comparing Christ Jesus to Judas. With
infinite patience, Christ Jesus bore all His suffering and torture
until the moment when He finally released His spirit and turned
it over to the hands of the divine Father. (See Luke 23:46.) In
absolute polarity to this is the end of Judas' life where, to his
betrayal, suicide was added.[70] Thus, the greatest contrast to
Christ Jesus is placed for all eternity before humankind through
Judas' tragic destiny.

Concerning the Nature of Christian Freedom

The right use of freedom is the central task for present-day
humanity. For precisely this is where the clear dividing line stands
between the Christian and luciferic experiences of freedom. The
first is expressed by Christ Himself in the statement: "And ye
shall know the truth, and the truth shall make you free" (John
8:32). Just the opposite occurs with suicide and with the support
for it. For this is not concerned with a knowledge of truth in the
higher sense—otherwise, every inclination to kill oneself would

be immediately rejected; it is concerned, rather, with a fateful deed that is performed only out of an inability or unwillingness to perceive the spiritual world and the present activity of Christ as Lord of Karma. And because such a deed lacks a connection to truth, it is, as already mentioned, unfree in the highest degree.

From this it follows that the final overcoming of the tendency for suicide in present-day humanity can only happen from two sources—from the realm of freedom and from that of truthfulness. Today people must gain knowledge about the nature of true Christian freedom, and at the same time become aware of the path upon which, in a modern way, cognition of truth is possible. And in the sense of the words of Christ just mentioned, this process cannot be separated from knowledge of the spiritual world.

These two possibilities were brought into the world by Rudolf Steiner, first in his early work *The Philosophy of Spiritual Activity* (GA 4), and then in the anthroposophy founded by him.

Thus, we can ask at the end of these considerations: How does the ideal of the free human being described in *The Philosophy of Spiritual Activity*, who in this way seeks to achieve ethical individualism in life, relate to the whole problem of suicide and medical assistance for it? In my view, the answer must be: When it comes to pass that more people strive to realize ethical individualism on earth, then suicide will become impossible. For no matter the reason it is committed, it is a deed of the greatest un-freedom, and through it those individuals can become separated from their higher being. Ethical individualism and the real striving for it totally exclude suicide, as well as any tendency toward it.

And with regard to anthroposophy itself, its most important task involves raising an awareness of the reality of the spiritual world—its nature and its laws—to such an extent that a deed such as suicide is ruled out of human life. Rudolf Steiner says in this regard: "No one who sees the meaning of such a deed would carry it out. And when spiritual science really passes over into human perception, there will be no more suicide" (GA 175: February 20, 1917).

It is precisely anthroposophical medicine, which proceeds from a spiritual-scientific understanding of the world and humanity—with its strict orientation toward the preservation of every human life—that should raise its voice courageously regarding this question in order to ensure the Christian future of humankind. It is precisely in the current public discussion that anthroposophical doctors can make an important contribution toward the Christianizing of medicine, especially through their rich experiences in anthroposophical methods of treating and accompanying patients with the most difficult, even incurable illnesses.

Notes

References from the works of Rudolf Steiner given in the text and the following notes refer to the pages of the German editions (GA). All passages have been newly translated to give consistency of terminology.

1   Ernst Klee, *Euthanasie im NS-Staat*. Frankfurt 1993, p. 100/ German edition [hereafter "/G"].

2   Karl Binding, Alfred Hoche, *Die Freigabe der Vernichtung lebensunwerten Lebens. Ihr Mass und ihre Form*, Leipzig 1920. Cf. Contributions to Rudolf Steiner's Collected Works, Nr. 108, p. 51/G. (List of Rudolf Steiner's medical library.)

3   Rudolf Steiner: *Gegensätze in der Menschheitsentwicklung*, lecture in Stuttgart on March 9, 1920 (GA 197). Dornach 1967. In English: *Polarities in the Evolution of Mankind*, Rudolf Steiner Press 1987.

4   Compare this with the current occasion of Issue No. 5 of the magazine *Der Merkurstab*, Vol. 63, September/October 2010, which focuses on the theme "Assisted Suicide? Ethics of Dying in Anthroposophical Medicine."

5   Rudolf Steiner, *Physiologisch-Therapeutisches auf Grundlage der Geiseswissenschaft* [Physiology and Therapy Based on Spiritual Science] (GA 314). Dornach ³1989, p. 283/G. Fragments of this GA in English: *Physiology and Therapeutics*, Mercury Press; *Fundamentals of Anthroposophical Medicine: Four lectures to doctors*, Mercury Press 1986; and *Health Care as a Social Issue*, Mercury Press 1984.

6   Cf. Peter Selg: *Krankheit, Heilung und Schicksal des Menschen. Über Rudolf Steiners geisteswissenschaftliches Pathologie- und Therapieverständnis*, Dornach 2004.

7   Rudolf Steiner: *Natur und Mensch in geisteswissenschaftlicher Betrachtung* (GA 352). Dornach ³1981, p. 143/G. Fragments in English: *From Elephants to Einstein* (10 discussions with workers), Rudolf Steiner Press 1998.

8 Christoph Wilhelm Hufeland: "Die Verhältnisse des Arztes." In: *Hufelands Journal*, No. 23, 1806, p. 15f./G, italics P. Selg.

9 Rudolf Steiner: *Heilpädagogischer Kurs.* (GA 317). Dornach ⁸1995, p. 61/G. In English: *Education for Special Needs: The Curative Education Course*, Rudolf Steiner Press 1998.

10 Willem Zeylmans van Emmichoven: "Rudolf Steiner in Holland." In: M.J. Krück von Poturzyn (Ed.): *Wir erlebten Rudolf Steiner. Erinnerungen seiner Schüler.* Stuttgart ³1967, p. 257/G.

11 Rudolf Steiner: *Meditative Betrachtungen und Anleitungen zur Vertiefung der Heilkunst* (GA 316). Dornach ⁴2003, p. 122/G. In English: *Course for Young Doctors*, Mercury Press 1997.

12 *Ibid.*, p. 220/G.

13 Rudolf Steiner: *Die Offenbarungen des Karma* (GA 120). Dornach ⁸1992, p. 90f./G; italics P. Selg. In English: *Manifestations of Karma*, Rudolf Steiner Press 2011.

14 Rudolf Steiner: *Das Prinzip der spirituellen Ökonomie* (GA 109). Dornach ³2000, p. 160/G. In English: *The Principle of Spiritual Economy*, Rudolf Steiner Press 1986.

15 Cf. *Note 9*.

16 For this, Cf. especially Rudolf Steiner's lectures from May 24, 1924 and June 8, 1924 (GA 239). In English: *Karmic Relationships: Esoteric Studies Vol. 5*, Rudolf Steiner Press 2011.

17 Rudolf Steiner: *Die Weihnachtstagung zur Begrundung der Allgemeinen Anthroposophischen Gesellschaft 1923/24* (GA 260). Dornach 1994, p. 35/G. In English: *The Christmas Conference for the Foundation of the General Anthroposophical Society 1923-1924*, Anthroposophic Press 199.

18 Cf. Peter Selg: *Krankheit und Christus-Erkenntnis. Anthroposophische Medizin als christliche Heilkunst.* Dornach ¹2001; und Peter Selg: *Christliche Medizin. Die ideellen Beziehungen des Christentums zur Heilkunde und die Anthroposophische Medizin.* Dornach 2005.

19 Cf. Peter Selg: "Ita Wegman and the 'Courage to Heal.'" In: *Der Merkurstab*. Vol. 4, 2008, pp. 362-369/G.

20 Cited after Peter Selg: "Vom Umgang mit dem Tod. Ein Beitrag zur ärztlichen Gesinnung Ita Wegmans." In: *Der Merkurstab*. Vol. 2, 2006, p. 5/G.

21 Translation from Ancient Greek. This text is taken from *Wikipedia*,

search word "Hippocratic Oath," where the "classic translation" from Ludwig Edelstein, Owsei Temkin, and C. Lilian Temkin (Ed.), *Ancient Medicine*, Johns Hopkins University Press 1987, p. 6 is presented. Inasmuch as the fifth section is missing in this translation, this text is added from the "original, translated into English" according to "The Hippocratic Oath," by Michael North, National Library of Medicine, National Institutes of Health.

22 GA 178: November 16, 1917. In English: *Secret Brotherhoods: And the Mystery of the Human Double*, Rudolf Steiner Press 2011; and *Geographic Medicine: The Secret of the Double*, Mercury Press 1986.

23 In his lecture about Paracelsus (1493–1541), Rudolf Steiner points out how this old, traditional medicine seeks to develop further out of the knowledge of its time. Therefore, for [Paracelsus], Hippocrates represented a great ideal that was hardly achievable anymore. "The father of medicine, Hippocrates, represented for him a great ideal. Today's scholar can neither fulfill what that Greek was, nor what Paracelsus saw in him." (GA 54: April 26, 1906; not translated.) For the capability Hippocrates possessed, and what Paracelsus also tried to develop in himself later, "was the intuitive view, which did not begin with the physical, but with the finer *etheric* underlying the corporeal" (*ibid.*). And "Paracelsus had taken into himself the spirit of such an intuitive medicine," (*ibid.*) whereby he became the most famous doctor of his time. Therefore, he is part of Hippocrates' medical stream. (For more detail about Paracelsus from the anthroposophical point of view, see Peter Selg: *Michael und Christus. Studien zur Anthroposophie Rudolf Steiners*, Chapter 4, "Die Heilung des Menschen. Rudolf Steiner und Paracelsus." Arlesheim 2010.) The etheric aspect mentioned here comprises in human beings, as well as in nature, the most comprehensive foundation of life. Therefore, the greatest esteem for every human life is the fundamental medical Mystery ethic, which was also found condensed in the Hippocratic Oath. Rudolf Steiner explained with the following comparison how Hippocrates could see super-sensible influences behind the material appearance of the physical-sensory body: "When in a chemical laboratory today you see an alembic, under which there is a flame, and you see the product of

the material inside—just as diaphanous is the effect of the soul-spiritual in the bodily fluids—just as transparent, super-sensibly lucent, was for Hippocrates what happened in human beings." (GA 204: June 5, 1921. In English: *Materialism and the Task of Anthroposophy*, Anthroposophic Press 1987.)

24   The Hippocratic writings, together with those that are considered to be composed by him, are known as the "Corpus Hippocraticum" and consist of around 60 works, which were written during the period of the fifth century B.C. until the first century A.D.

25   Hippocrates, in transforming medical Mystery-knowledge into the thought-forms that were developed at that time by Greek philosophers, always remained strictly true to the original source of his knowledge. Therefore, Rudolf Steiner characterizes him as representative of the original, *still instinctive medicine*, which drew more upon suprasensible observations than on intellectual reasoning. (The latter was subsequently introduced into medical science, especially by the Roman doctor Galen [131 – 201 A.D.].) "As far as one can trace, it is known ... that for Hippocrates the last offshoots of an old instinctive medicine outweighed the mere beginning of today's intellectual medicine." (GA 314: April 7, 1920. In English: see *Note 5, op. cit.*).

26   Renouncing abortions was not a matter of a formal or moral prohibition, rather it was based on a deep knowledge about the prenatal life of the human soul. Rudolf Steiner mentioned in many lectures what that really means. (For this see Peter Selg: *Unbornness: Human Pre-existence and the Journey toward Birth*, SteinerBooks 2010.).

27   That this passage refers directly to the misuse of children emerges from the parallel section of the Matthew Gospel: "At the same time came the disciples unto Jesus, saying, Who is the greatest in the kingdom of heaven? And Jesus called a little child unto him, and set him in the midst of them, and said, Verily I say unto you, Except you be converted, and become as little children, ye shall not enter into the kingdom of heaven. Whosoever therefore shall humble himself as this little child, the same is greatest in the kingdom of heaven. And whoso shall receive one such little child in my name receiveth me. But whoso shall offend one of

these little ones which believe in me, it were better for him that a millstone were hung around his neck, and that he were drowned in the depth of the sea" (Matthew 18:1-6). Compared with the comprehensive formulation in the Luke Gospel, this refers particularly to children who believe in Christ. In this connection, sexual offences toward children in religious communities and institutions must be considered especially abysmal. Also in the Mark Gospel such an offence is judged in similar words. It is additionally mentioned that when summoning children, Christ "took them in His arms" (Mark 9:36), in order to emphasize once again the special love and concern heavenly beings have for them.

28   See Rudolf Steiner: *The Spiritual Guidance of the Individual and Humanity* (GA 15), Chapter I, Anthroposophic Press 1992.

29   Therefore, the girl, who in the novel *Demons* (supplementary chapter "With Tichon") by F. M. Dostoyevsky was seduced and sexually abused by Stavrogin, says the heart-rending words: "I have killed God [in me]."

30   Regarding Sorat as Antichrist and cosmic opponent of Christ, see Rudolf Steiner: *The Apocalypse of St. John* (GA 104), June 29, 1908, Rudolf Steiner Press 1985.

31   In order to make understandable the fine distinction between the form of the human body and its material aspect, Rudolf Steiner would often use an example in his lectures that the scholastic philosophers applied in the Middle Ages: Through metabolic processes the material that makes up a human body is completely exchanged over a time period of approximately seven years. In animals this occurs much faster. In this sense, if a person were to feed a wolf for a corresponding period of its life only with lamb meat, it would consist after awhile only of lamb-matter. However, a wolf could never turn into a lamb in this way—the form, which controls the material in it, does not permit such an alteration.

32   Friedrich Schiller, *Complete Works*, Volume 1, p. 201/G; italics Schiller, Darmstadt 1987. Regarding this, see also S.O. Prokofieff, *Friedrich Schiller und die Zukunft der Freiheit. Zugleich einige Aspekte seiner okkulten Biographie*, Dornach 2007. [Friedrich Schiller and the Future of Freedom. Several Aspects of His Occult Biography]; not yet translated.

33   In this regard, it is apparent that one was still fully conscious of this problem in the older Egyptian mysteries. With mummification, in order to remove the soft parts of the body, the form necessarily had to be harmed. This could not be performed by a priest, who otherwise carried out the embalming and participated in the Mystery rituals. Therefore, in Egypt special people from the lowest class were designated for that. At the beginning of the embalming process, one of them ran into the hall where this was to occur and made a little cut with a knife in the dead person's body, whereupon he had to leave the room as quickly as possible while the priests scolded and threatened him. For them, it was a crime to encroach upon the human form in this manner. However, after it was lacerated, they could properly prepare the body for embalming..

34   In the Eastern tradition, Kali Yuga (in English "Dark Age") means the time period in the history of humankind in which the old Mystery-wisdom had to retreat increasingly so that humankind could achieve the freedom and independence of the individuality..

35   See Rudolf Steiner's statement cited in *Note 25.*

36   In this regard, see Peter Selg, *Ich bleibe bei Ihnen. Rudolf Steiner und Ita Wegman. München, Whitsun 1907. Dornach, 1923-1925,* Stuttgart 2007.

37   See, above all, the book written by Rudolf Steiner and Ita Wegman together: *Fundamentals of Therapy* (GA 27), Mercury Press 2010.

38   In Europe the Hippocratic Oath was replaced after World War II by the so-called "Physician's Pledge" (also known as the "Geneva Pledge"), which despite its different wording contains some aspects of the original oath; thus, for example, the following statement: "I will maintain the utmost respect for human life, from the time of its conception." (*Wikipedia,* according to the World Medical Association Council Meeting in Paris, May 8-10, 1997.) This has since been amended simply to: "I will maintain the utmost respect for human life." (*Wikipedia,* according to the World Medical Association International Code of Medical Ethics.)

39   Some of these publications are listed at the end of this book in "Further Literature Regarding the Topic."

40   See in this regard, the spiritual-scientific suggestions that Rudolf Steiner gave to educators, healing educators, pharmacists, bankers, farmers, artists, theologians, and natural scientists.

41   In this regard, Rudolf Steiner says materialism in humankind will increase further until the middle of the Fifth Post-Atlantean epoch, which will be reached in the year 2,463..

42   Albert Steffen: *Meetings with Rudolf Steiner*, Dornach 1975.

43   Even in a fatal accident, when death occurs just as fast for those suddenly affected, the negative results—because this event is set in the person's destiny—are compensated for by the higher (hierarchical) beings of the spiritual world, which rule over karma. However, such compensation is not possible in suicide, so that after death the person's soul must accept and suffer from all the negative results proceeding from it.

44   The desperate after-death situation of a person who commits suicide—which Rudolf Steiner describes here from his spiritual research—is confirmed many times in the widespread literature today dealing with after-death experiences..

45   In a later lecture, Rudolf Steiner speaks again about the "elementary spirits of birth and death," which are "messengers of Ahriman" and are exceptionally hostile toward everything that happens with and among human beings. (See GA 177: October 6, 1917. In English: *The Fall of the Spirits of Darkness*, Rudolf Steiner Press 1995.) The hierarchies need these spirits, however, in order to control the processes of birth and death. These elemental spirits remain within the bounds of their necessary functions concerning the spiritual-earthly household as long as human birth and death happen in harmony with divine guidance. If this is breached, then these spirits have the opportunity to go beyond the boundaries established for them and take possession of human beings.

46   In a later lecture, Rudolf Steiner speaks again about the "elementary spirits of birth and death," which are "messengers of Ahriman" and are exceptionally hostile toward everything that happens with and among human beings. (See GA 177: October 6, 1917. In English: *The Fall of the Spirits of Darkness*, Rudolf Steiner Press 1995.) The hierarchies need these spirits, however, in order to control the processes of birth and death. These elemental spirits remain within the bounds of their necessary

functions concerning the spiritual-earthly household as long as human birth and death happen in harmony with divine guidance. If this is breached, then these spirits have the opportunity to go beyond the boundaries established for them and take possession of human beings.

47   Cited after Maria von Nagy: *Rudolf Steiner über den Selbstmord*, Dornach 1998. [Rudolf Steiner on Suicide.]

48   There are undoubtedly many encounters with Christ at the moment of death of which the outer world knows nothing, especially for those people killed in war or in concentration camps, who often had to die under unimaginably terrible conditions.

49   In this regard, see the description about Friedrich Schiller's moment of death in S.O. Prokofieff: *Friedrich Schiller und die Zukunft der Freiheit* (See Note 32, *op. cit.*), Chapter II, Section 3: "Schiller's Premature Death and Its Spiritual-Historical Results."

50   The "World Midnight Hour," in spiritual science, designates the highest point of the path that the human soul reaches in the spiritual world between two incarnations. This name was chosen because the individuality at this point in after-death existence awakens to the cosmic aspect of the level of consciousness that he possessed on earth only in a completely unconscious way during the state of deep, dreamless sleep.

51   This is so because the Mystery of Golgotha took place on earth; hence the relationship to it, and thereby also to Christ Himself, can be found only on the earth.

52   Regarding this, see Rudolf Steiner: *The Reappearance of Christ in the Etheric* (GA 118), Anthroposophic Press 2003.

53   Maria von Nagy, op. cit. *Note 47.*

54   See Maria von Nagy, op. cit. *Note 47.*

55   Regarding the fact that Christ always works in harmony with the spiritual powers of the entire cosmos, see *The Spiritual Guidance of the Individual and Humanity* (GA 15), (See Note 28, *op. cit.*); Chapter III.

56   The full text of the mantric verse is:

There in the brightness
I feel
the force of life.

Death awakens me
from sleep,
from spiritual sleep.

I will be
and make out of myself
what the illuminating power
radiates into me."

There emerges from the middle-sentence of the verse the fact
that the reflection upon the moment of death, hindered by suicide, leads to a weakening of "I"-consciousness after death; this
will be the topic of the next section.

57   In any case, the soul cannot continue in the spiritual world until
the actual point of death as determined by its destiny, has been
reached. Until this moment of its after-death existence, because
it is not able to connect to the spiritual world (the hierarchical
cosmos), the danger for the soul of being delivered to the ahrimanic spirits is especially great.

58   Regarding this, see the article by Rudolf Steiner in
Anthroposophical Leading Thoughts (GA 26), Rudolf Steiner
Press 2007: "What Is Revealed When a Person Reviews the
Previous Life between Death and a New Birth?"; first and second
parts.

59   Autobiographical lecture held in Berlin on February 4, 1913.
Published in the collection: Rudolf Steiner: *Selbstzeugnisse.
Autobiographische Dokumente*, Dornach 2007. In English: *Self-
Education: Autobiographical Reflections*, Mercury Press..

60   About the culture of selflessness so necessary for our time, see
Peter Selg: *The Culture of Selflessness. Rudolf Steiner, The Fifth
Gospel, and the Time of Extremes*, SteinerBooks 2012.

61   In the lecture of October 7, 1911 (GA 131), Rudolf Steiner says
that this activity of Christ as Lord of Karma *will begin at the end
of the twentieth century* ("around the end of the twentieth century"). In: *From Jesus to Christ*, Rudolf Steiner Press 2005.

62   Out of this relationship of Christ to *everyone* who goes through
the gate of death—no matter to which religion they belong (if
any)—the true greatness of Christianity can be recognized.
Therefore, Rudolf Steiner can say of it: "For Christianity was,

to be sure, a religion at the beginning; but Christianity is greater than all religions! ... The religious principle of Christianity in its beginning was more comprehensive than the religious principles of all other religions. But Christianity is greater still than the religious principle itself" (GA 102: March 24, 1908. In English: *The Festivals and Their Meaning*, Rudolf Steiner Press 2005).

63   In this sense, seen from a spiritual point of view, it is uncalled-for to use the term "free death" so as to glorify suicide.

64   Regarding such an idea of compulsion, which can emerge out of human thinking, Rudolf Steiner writes in *The Philosophy of Spiritual Activity*: "One must be able to confront oneself with the idea experientially; *otherwise*, one will become its slave" (GA 4, p. 271/G; italics Rudolf Steiner). In this case, such "slavery" can even lead to suicide. (See *Works Cited* for English publishing information.).

65   Rudolf Steiner visited Christian Morgenstern for the last time at the beginning of January 1914, almost three months before his death. At this time, the poet's illness (tuberculosis) was so advanced that he could hardly speak.

66   From the lecture of September 20, 1914; published in Rudolf Steiner: *Christian Morgenstern. Der Sieg des Lebens über den Tod* [The Victory of Life over Death], Dornach 1935; italics Rudolf Steiner.

67   See the previous footnote and Peter Selg: *Christian Morgenstern. Sein Weg mit Rudolf Steiner*, Stuttgart 2008.

68   From *Wir fanden einen Pfad. Neue Gedicht*, Munich 1917. In English: *We Have Found a Path. New Poems*, Mercury Press.

69   Conveyed by A. Arenson; italics Arenson. From an unpublished note.

70   Rudolf Steiner speaks about Judas Iscariot working in Ahriman's service in *The Fifth Gospel* (GA 148), October 6, 1913. Rudolf Steiner Press 2012.

Bibliography

Works of Rudolf Steiner Cited

AP = *Anthroposophic Press*
RSP = *Rudolf Steiner Press*
MP = *Mercury Press*
SB = *SteinerBooks*

GA 4   *The Philosophy of Spiritual Activity*, Tr. W. Lindeman, AP 1986 (repr. 2007). *The Philosophy of Freedom*, Tr. M. Wilson, RSP 1964 (repr. 2011). *Intuitive Thinking as a Spiritual Path*, Tr. M. Lipson, AP 1995.

GA 13   *An Outline of Occult Science*, Tr. H. Monges, AP 1972. *Occult Science: An Outline*, Tr. G. & M. Adams, RSP (repr. 2011). *An Outline of Esoteric Science*, Tr. C. Creeger, AP 1997.

GA 15   *The Spiritual Guidance of the Individual and Humanity*, Tr. S. Desch, AP 1992.

GA 26   *Anthroposophical Leading Thoughts*, Tr. G. & M. Adams, RSP 1973 (repr. 2007).

GA 27   *Fundamentals of Therapy*, Tr. C. van Tellingen, MP 2010. *Extending Practical Medicine*, Tr. A.R. Meuss, RSP 1997 (repr. 2001).

GA 54   *Die Welträtsel und die Anthroposophie* [World Mysteries and Anthroposophy] – not translated.

GA 93a   *Fundamentals of Esotericism*, RSP 1983.

GA 94   *An Esoteric Cosmology*, SB (repr. 2008).

GA 95   *Founding a Science of the Spirit*, Tr. revised: M. Barton, RSP 1999.

GA 102 *Das Hereinwirken geistiger Wesenheiten in den Menschen* [The Interweaving of Spiritual Beings in the Life of Humanity] – Fragments in: *The Festivals and Their Meaning*, Tr. revised: M. Barton, RSP 2008.

GA 104   *The Apocalypse of St. John: Lectures on the Book of Revelation*, RSP 1977, (repr. 1985).

GA 109   *The Principle of Spiritual Economy: In Connection with Questions of Reincarnation*, Tr. P. Mollenhauer, RSP 1986.

GA 118   *The Reappearance of Christ in the Etheric*, (Tr. various), AP 2003.

GA 120   *Manifestations of Karma*, Tr. H. Hermann-Davy, RSP (repr. 2011).

GA 130   *Esoteric Christianity: and the Mission of Christian Rosenkreutz*, Tr. P. Wehrle, RSP 1984 (repr. 2001).

GA 131   *From Jesus to Christ*, Tr. C. Davy, RSP (repr. 2005).

GA 143   *Erfahrungen des Übersinnlichen. Die drei Wege der Seele zu Christus* [Experiences of the Suprasensory. Three Ways of the Soul to Christ] – Fragments in: *Anthroposophy in Everyday Life*, (Tr. various), AP 1995.

GA 144   *The Mysteries of the East and of Christianity*, RSP 1972.

GA 148   *The Fifth Gospel: From the Akashic Record*, Tr. A.R. Meuss, revised: D. Osmond, C. Davy, RSP 1995, (repr. 2012).

GA 153   *The Inner Nature of Man: And Our Life Between Death and Rebirth*, Tr. A. Meuss, RSP 1995.

GA 157   *The Destinies of Individuals and of Nations*, RSP 1990.

GA 175   *Building Stones for a Realization of the Mystery of Golgotha: Cosmic and Human Metamorphosis*, Tr. A. H. Parker, RSP 1972.

GA 177   *The Fall of the Spirit of Darkness*, Tr. A.R. Meuss, RSP (repr. 2008).

GA 178   *Secret Brotherhoods: And the Mystery of the Human Double*, Tr. J. Collis, RSP (repr. 2011).

GA 182   *Death as Metamorphosis of Life*, Tr. S. Seiler, SB 2008.

GA 183   *Die Wissenschaft vom Werden des Menschen* [The Science of the Development of the Human Being] – not translated.

GA 197   *Polarities in the Evolution of Mankind*, RSP 1987.

GA 204   *Materialism and the Task of Anthroposophy*, Tr. M. St Goar, RSP 1987.

GA 206   *Man as a Being of Sense and Perception*, Anthroposophical Publishing Co. 1958.

GA 226   *Man's Being, His Destiny, and World Evolution*, Tr. E. McArthur, AP 1984.

GA 237   *Karmic Relationships: Esoteric Studies*, Vol. 3, Tr. G. Adams & D.S. Osmond, RSP (repr. 2002).

GA 239 *Karmic Relationships: Esoteric Studies,* Vol. 5, Tr. D.S. Osmond, RSP (repr. 2011).

GA 260 *The Christmas Conference: For the Foundation of the General Anthroposophical Society, 1923/1924,* Tr. J. Collis & M. Wilson, AP 1990.

GA 260a *The Foundation Stone / The Life, Nature & Cultivation of Anthroposophy,* RSP (repr. 2011).

GA 268 *Mantrische Sprüche. Seelenübungen. Band II, 1903-1925* [Soul Exercises: vol. 2: Mantric Verses, 1903–1925] – Fragments in *Breathing the Spirit,* Tr. M. Barton, Sophia Books 2002.

GA 314 Fragments in: *Physiology and Therapeutics,* MP; *Fundamentals of Anthroposophical Medicine* (Four Lectures to Doctors), MP 1986; and *Health Care as a Social Issue,* MP 1984.

GA 316 *Course for Young Doctors,* MP 1997.

GA 317 *Education for Special Needs: The Curative Education Course,* RSP 1998.

GA 318 *Broken Vessels: The Spiritual Structure of Human Frailty* (The Pastoral Medicine Course), AP (repr. 2003).

GA 352 *From Elephants to Einstein* (10 discussions with workers), RSP 1998.

Further Literature in German, not translated

Maria von Nagy: *Rudolf Steiner über den Selbstmord,* Dornach 1991.

Armin Husemann: *Euthanasie,* Stuttgart 1996.

Michaela Glöckler (Ed.): *Spirituelle Ethik. Situationsgerechtes, selbstverantwortetes Handeln,* Dornach 2002.

Publications of the Medical Section at the Goetheanum

Michaela Glöckler, Rolf Heine (Eds.): "Ethik des Sterbens – Würde des Lebens. Geistige, rechtliche und wirtschaftliche Fragen zum Altwerden, Sterben und nachtodlichen Leben," *Persephone,* Vol. 1, Dornach 2000.

Michaela Glöckler, Rolf Heine (Eds.): "Handeln im Umkreis des Todes. Praktische Hinweise für die Pflege des Körpers, die Aufbahrung, die spirituelle Begleitung des Verstorbenen," *Persephone,* Vol. 4, Dornach 2003.

Books in English Translation by
Peter Selg

ON RUDOLF STEINER:

Rudolf Steiner and Christian Rosenkreutz

*Rudolf Steiner as a Spiritual Teacher: From Recollections of
Those Who Knew Him*

ON CHRISTOLOGY:

The Creative Power of Anthroposophical Christology
(with Sergei Prokofieff)

Christ and the Disciples: The Destiny of an Inner Community

*Rudolf Steiner and the Fifth Gospel: Insights into a New
Understanding of the Christ Mystery*

*The Figure of Christ: Rudolf Steiner and the Spiritual Intention
behind the Goetheanum's Central Work of Art*

Seeing Christ in Sickness and Healing

ON GENERAL ANTHROPOSOPHY:

*The Culture of Selflessness: Rudolf Steiner, the Fifth Gospel,
and the Time of Extremes*

*The Mystery of the Heart: The Sacramental Physiology of the
Heart in Aristotle, Thomas Aquinas, and Rudolf Steiner*

*Rudolf Steiner and the School for Spiritual Science
The Foundation of the First Class*

*The Fundamental Social Law: Rudolf Steiner on the Work of
the Individual and the Spirit of Community*

*The Agriculture Course, Koberwitz, Whitsun 1924: Rudolf
Steiner and the Beginnings of Biodynamics*

The Path of the Soul after Death: The Community of the Living and the Dead as Witnessed by Rudolf Steiner in his Eulogies and Farewell Addresses

Rudolf Steiner's Intentions for the Anthroposophical Society: The Executive Council, the School for Spiritual Science, and the Sections

ON ANTHROPOSOPHICAL MEDICINE AND CURATIVE EDUCATION:

I am for going ahead: Ita Wegman's Work for the Social Ideals of Anthroposophy

Karl König: The Child with Special Needs: Letters and Essays on Curative Education (Ed.)

Ita Wegman and Karl König: Letters and Documents

Karl König: My Task: Autobiography and Biographies (Ed.)

Karl König's Path to Anthroposophy

ON CHILD DEVELOPMENT AND WALDORF EDUCATION:

I Am Different from You: How Children Experience Themselves and the World in the Middle of Childhood

The Essence of Waldorf Education

Unbornness: Human Pre-existence and the Journey toward Birth

A Grand Metamorphosis: Contributions to the Spiritual-Scientific Anthropology and Education of Adolescents

The Therapeutic Eye: How Rudolf Steiner Observed Children

BIOGRAPHIES:

The Last Three Years: Ita Wegman in Ascona, 1940--1943

From Gurs to Auschwitz: The Inner Journey of Maria Krehbiel-Darmstadter

Ita Wegman Institute
for Basic Research into Anthroposophy
Pfeffinger Weg 1 A CH-4144 Arlesheim, Switzerland
www.wegmaninstitut.ch
e-mail: sekretariat@wegmaninstitut.ch

The Ita Wegman Institute for Basic Research into Anthroposophy is a non-profit research and teaching organization. It undertakes basic research into the lifework of Dr. Rudolf Steiner (1861–1925) and the application of Anthroposophy in specific areas of life, especially medicine, education, and curative education. The Institute also contains and cares for the literary estates of Ita Wegman, Madeleine van Deventer, Hilma Walter, Willem Zeylmans van Emmichoven, Karl Schubert, and others. Work carried out by the Institute is supported by a number of foundations and organizations and an international group of friends and supporters. The Director of the Institute is Prof. Dr. Peter Selg.